Pineapple Quilts

New Quilts from an Old Favorite

edited by Barbara Smith

American Quilter's Society

P.O.Box 3290 • Paducah, KY 42002-3290

Located in Paducah, Kentucky, the American Quilter's Society (AQS), is dedicated to promoting the accomplishments of today's quilters. Through its publications and events, AQS strives to honor today's quiltmakers and their work — and inspire future creativity and innovation in quiltmaking.

EDITOR: BARBARA SMITH
BOOK DESIGN/ILLUSTRATIONS: ELAINE WILSON
COVER DESIGN: JUSTIN GREEN
PHOTOGRAPHY: CHARLES R. LYNCH

Library of Congress Cataloging-in-Publication Data
Pineapple quilts : new quilts from an old favorite / edited by Barbara Smith.
p.cm.
ISBN 1-57432-711-9
1. Patchwork. 2. Quilting. 3. Patchwork--Patterns. 4. Quilting--Patterns. 5. Pineapple in art. 6. Quilting--Competitions--United States. I. Smith, Barbara, 1941– . II. American Quilter's Society.
TT835.P558   1998
746.46'041--dc21   98-16426
                                                             CIP

Additional copies of this book may be ordered from American Quilter's Society, PO Box 3290, Paducah, KY 42002-3290 @ $16.95. Add $2.00 for postage & handling.

Printed in the U.S.A. by Image Graphics, Paducah, KY

Dedication

This book is dedicated to quiltmakers of all
times and all places, whose works continue
to inspire and delight.

Contents

Preface

This book was developed in conjunction with the annual Museum of the American Quilter's Society (MAQS) contest and exhibit called "New Quilts from Old Favorites." Dedicated to honoring today's quilters, MAQS created this contest to recognize, and share with others, the many fascinating interpretations that can grow out of a single traditional quilt block.

A brief description of the contest is followed by a presentation of the 18 finalists and their quilts, including the five award winners. Full-color photographs of the quilts accompany the quiltmakers' comments, which provide fascinating insights into the creative process. Full-size templates of the traditional Pineapple block, and tips, techniques, and patterns contributed by the contest winners are provided so that you, too, will be able to enjoy making your own Pineapple quilt.

It is our hope that this combination of outstanding quilts, full-size patterns, and instructions will inspire as many exciting quilts as the original contest did, adding new contributions to this pattern's continuing tradition.

For information about entering the current year's contest, write to MAQS, PO Box 1540, Paducah, KY 42002-1540.

Sponsors

A special thanks goes to the corporations whose generous support
has made this contest, exhibit, and book possible:

The Contest

This publication grows out of an annual international contest, called "New Quilts from Old Favorites," sponsored by the Museum of the American Quilter's Society. Each year, the contest challenges quiltmakers to develop innovative quilts from a different traditional pattern. The theme for 1998 was the Pineapple block.

The only design requirement for quilts entered in the contest was that the quilt be recognizable in some way as being related to the Pineapple. The quilt also had to be a minimum of 50" in each dimension and not exceed 100" in any one dimension, and it had to be quilted. A quilt could only be entered by the person who made it, and it had to have been complete after December 31, 1992. Many exciting interpretations of the pattern were submitted by quilters from around the world. From these entries, 18 quilts were selected, which are featured in this publication and a traveling exhibition.

The Pineapple Block

The Pineapple block, also known as Maltese Cross, Windmill Blades, and Church Steps, is a variation of the Log Cabin. In early times, the block was frequently sewn on a muslin foundation. This intriguing pattern looks intimidating, but paper-foundation piecing has removed the difficulty, making this versatile block accessible to quilters of all skill levels.

The design is usually created by alternating light and dark "blades." Each blade can be all one color, or it can be striped with alternating values of light and dark. The logs can be arranged so that rings form around the block. These rings can be regularly or randomly spaced. The center square (or diamond) and the logs can vary in width and length, and while a red center is traditional for Log Cabins, you can use any color you like.

The contestants have introduced some fascinating design variations to the original Pineapple quilt concept. Several entries contain distorted Pineapple blocks, featuring elongated rectangles, curved piecing, or irregular logs. Some winning designs drew their strength from unusual color placement in the blades, while others successfully combined simple blocks, such as Nine Patches and Starts, with the traditional Pineapple. Appliqué was also used effectively to enhance several of the quilts.

It is hoped that, as you view the beautiful and exciting quilts in these pages, you will be inspired to make a Pineapple quilt or perhaps design some Pineapple variations of your own.

The Winners

FIRST PLACE

Mary Ann Herndon
Houston, Texas
PAINTED PINEAPPLE

SECOND PLACE

Dixie Haywood
Pensacola, Florida
WEBSITE

THIRD PLACE

Judy Sogn
Seattle, Washington
CRUSHED PINEAPPLE

FOURTH PLACE

Sherri Bain Driver
Englewood, Colorado
PINEAPPLE SALSA

FIFTH PLACE

Jane C. Hall
Raleigh, North Carolina
CHROMA VI: NEBULA

and Their Quilts

FINALISTS

Marta Amundson

Shirley Robinson Davis

Mary Esson Dowling

Gertrude S. Embree & M. Gayle Wallace

Armida R. James

Linda Juniér

Patricia Klem

Lois Monieson

Anne J. Oliver

Elizabeth Rymer

Ida M. Tendam

Joan Will

Adrienne Yorinks

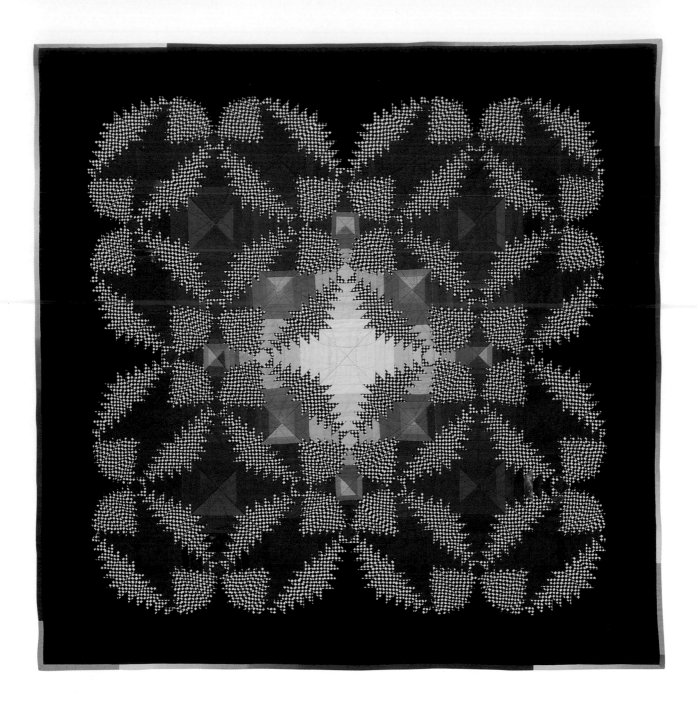

Painted Pineapple

64" x 64", 1997
Cotton fabric and batting
Machine pieced, hand quilted

Mary Ann Herndon
Houston, Texas

MY QUILTING

Yvonne Porcella was the speaker at my first Houston Quilt Guild meeting over 15 years ago. Her presentation was so dynamic that, from that point on, I was hooked. I'd always enjoyed fabric art, such as needlepoint, embroidery, or sewing, but finding time for quilting has eliminated any time for all my past fabric pursuits.

I am in awe of the many quilters who have influenced my work. It's hard to narrow the list, but I would like to thank Jinny Beyer and her genius for geometry and design; Yvonne Porcella and her vivid color sense; Allison Goss and her innovative use of color and design; Paula Nadelstern and her unbelievable kaleidoscopes. These quilt artists have all helped me to expand my quilting visions. Another large source of inspiration for me has been the art in children's books. For most of my working life, I was a school librarian and then became director of a library system. During that time, I had the opportunity to review all the new children's books published each year. Some of the best art around is in them.

I love entering contests, and since I retired last year, I have a lot more time to concentrate on creating fabric art so that I can participate in shows and contests.

MY PINEAPPLE QUILT

For my quilt, I had two yards of a fabric that shaded from yellow to purple, and I knew immediately that I would use it to fan out from the middle. My decisions to use the check and the block border were influenced by a quilt by Pamela Studstill. If I were to do it again, I would start sooner, and I would try to design a block with fewer logs. I really wanted to machine quilt PAINTED PINEAPPLE, but after a few tries, I realized that I needed to improve my machine quilting before embarking on such a project.

Since I couldn't find a commercial off-center 10" Pineapple block, I designed one. Before enlarging it to the 10" size and duplicating it, I tried shading it in various ways. I duplicated those designs many times and played with arrangements on my design board. The one I finally chose had the most movement.

It helped with the construction to have a master copy with the colors indicated. On each paper block, I labeled the colors on the logs because it was very easy to get mixed-up and put colors in the wrong places. Of course, when you do that, you lose your pattern. The quilting in the border was simply an extension of the Pineapple log lines, and various-sized circles were quilted in the body of the quilt.

> I find that fabric is the starting point for most of my quilts, and this one was no exception.

13

Website

53" x 53", 1997
Commercial and hand-dyed cotton fabrics, cotton batting
Machine pieced, hand quilted

Dixie Haywood
Pensacola, Florida

MY QUILTING

Even though I made a quilt for my first child 43 years ago, I did not really start quilting until nearly 15 years later, in the late 1960s. The person who influenced my work the most was a non-quilter my mother. She was a talented craftsman in thread and paint. She knew how to learn a skill and then expand it with imagination and innovation. Her example made me feel that the only limitations on what I could do were self-imposed.

Designing a quilt is exciting and challenging. Constructing it gives the gratification of progressively completing a task, often with enough problem solving along the way to keep things interesting.

I can never speak of a next project in the singular, since I always have several going at once, usually in the various stages of thinking, designing, construction, and quilting. I am spending half of next year quilting my daughter's wedding quilt, hopefully in time for her 13th anniversary. It's been a long-term project!

I have recently retired from teaching quiltmaking and plan to spend more time making quilts, writing, gardening, and enjoying life with my family.

MY PINEAPPLE QUILT

WEBSITE is the latest quilt in my series of Sliced Pineapples, which have logs made of more than one fabric. This quilt has sliced logs on the horizontal, vertical, and diagonal, arranged to form a spider-web graphic that appears imposed on an otherwise traditional Pineapple design. The web was formed by having the same fabric as the first slice on the horizontal and vertical planes and as the second slice on the diagonal planes.

The variegated hand-dyed fabric, pieced on the diagonal plane, forms the nine central stars that alternate with the yellow fabric forming the pineapples. A frame for the yellow and variegated images was formed by using the same fabric on all planes in the blocks at the quilt's edges. The web-like fabric used for the sliced webs within the quilt is also used in the corners at the outside edge of the pieced blocks and in the final border.

WEBSITE was machine pieced on temporary foundations made from tracing paper. Foundation piecing conquers potential technical problems by stabilizing the block. In addition, innovative variations are easier to piece without frustrating errors because you can mark the fabric and color choices on the foundations.

I have been fascinated for over 20 years by this classic pattern that achieves complexity with simple shapes.

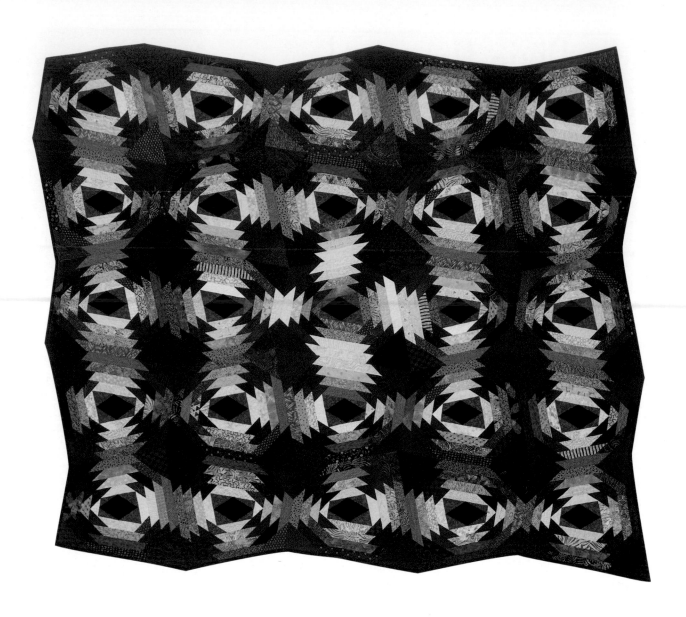

Crushed Pineapple

58" x 66", 1997
Cotton fabrics, polyester batting
Machine pieced and quilted

Judy Sogn
Seattle, Washington

MY QUILTING

My quilting life began in 1982, following interests in knitting and needlepoint. Wanting to make gifts for my family, I discovered projects that incidentally incorporated quilting techniques. Eventually, I realized I might be able to make an entire quilt. That thought grew, and today, I am totally immersed in quilts and quilting.

I make quilts because I love the entire process, from selecting fabrics and creating original designs, to finishing the binding by hand. Yes, I have even learned to tolerate basting because I know how important it is to my hand quilting. I do my machine piecing during the day, and I especially enjoy the challenge of intricate pieced designs. In the evening, I do my hand quilting while I am watching (mostly listening) to television with my husband. My machine quilting skills are limited, but developing. I was pleased to be able to machine quilt CRUSHED PINEAPPLE.

Currently, I am working on a joint project with my good friend Sue Linker. We are quilting the second team quilt that we have made for competition. We enjoy combining our separate skills and specialties and the shared camaraderie that develops on such big projects.

MY PINEAPPLE QUILT

I wanted my quilt to have jagged edges, and I felt that an irregular quadrilateral shape would accomplish that. I had no idea how to draft the pineapple in this shape, so I decided to "wing" it. I drew a large quadrilateral, being careful to avoid having any two sides parallel. An earlier attempt taught me that near-parallel sides in a block will produce two straight sides to the quilt.

Next, I drew lines within the block that were parallel to the sides and spaced at 1" intervals. The center area became a smaller irregular quadrilateral. I found the center of each side of this smaller shape and then connected the mid-points to form a diamond for the very center. Finally, I drew lines parallel to the sides of the diamond to form the logs in the corners.

I am a hand quilter by preference. However, there just wasn't time to hand quilt this one, so I machine stipple quilted with invisible thread over the entire quilt. I must admit the machine quilting was faster but, for me, not nearly as rewarding as the relaxing time I spend quilting by hand.

I find irregular quadrilaterals intriguing, and I thought they would make an interesting format for the Pineapple pattern.

17

Pineapple Salsa

64" x 64", 1997
Cotton fabrics
Machine pieced and quilted

Sherri Bain Driver
Englewood, Colorado

MY QUILTING

My mother and grandmother both made clothes, and I learned to love fabric long before I could sew. I remember sorting scraps into "families" and using cloth to make art projects just like other kids use crayons or paints. When I was eight, Mom taught me to use the sewing machine, and I made my clothes for many years. I made my first quilt when I was 19 and made a few more quilts in the next 15 years.

In 1987, I discovered quilt shops, quilt books, and quilt guilds, and I've been excited about quilt-making ever since. I'm fortunate to be able to be involved in some aspect of quiltmaking every day. It may be teaching, lecturing, designing, or sewing. I make some very traditional quilts, but what I really love is to take a traditional idea and change it in some way. I enter quite a few contests because they get the creative juices flowing and the deadline provides me with the incentive to finish.

MY PINEAPPLE QUILT

The fabrics I used were collected on various trips. Some came from far-away exotic vacations, some from local trips. I collect fabrics without a specific quilt in mind. I also sew pieces and parts of quilts without a total plan.

I began PINEAPPLE SALSA several years ago when I was experimenting with making eight-pointed stars from an interesting ikat fabric. I was pleased with the results, but since I didn't have a plan for the rest of the quilt, I put the pieces away and waited for inspiration. When I heard that MAQS had chosen the Pineapple block for their annual contest, I began playing with the idea of incorporating my ikat stars into a Pineapple design.

After making a rough sketch, I drafted Pineapple blocks to accommodate the stars and other hand-woven and ikat fabrics. The blocks were paper pieced, and the central star was set in. Border pieces were drafted and templates were made to fit the odd-sized blocks and to use the design of each fabric to its best advantage. The striped fabric that forms God's eyes was cut from a discarded robe that had belonged to my husband.

In several places, I ran out of a fabric. I used to think this was a terrible problem, but now I view it as an opportunity to make my quilts much more interesting.

Chroma VI: Nebula

58" x 58", 1997
Sueded cotton fabrics, polyester batting
Machine pieced, hand and machine quilted

Jane C. Hall
Raleigh, North Carolina

MY QUILTING

I cannot imagine not making more Pineapple designs. As soon as I work on something else, a fabric speaks to me and says "Pineapple!" I envision several more colorwash Pineapples, but I have also made a traditionally colored Pineapple bed quilt, inspired by an antique quilt. I constantly change the Pineapple design. I may change the shape or orientation of the center, the corners, the borders, and the overall design. There are not enough hours or days to make them all.

I have always done handwork, but didn't begin quilting until I saw a Hawaiian quilt when we lived in Hawaii in the late 1960s. It took a year to make, and I was hooked.

I am heavily involved in quiltmaking, and I love what I do. I work by hand and by machine, often in the same piece. I teach, judge, and appraise quilts, and collect both antique and contemporary quilts.

My next project is another colorwash Pineapple quilt. I have a sea theme in mind, and the fabric ready to work with. All I need is some time to think and plan and then cut and sew. I am also exploring all the different ways to work with off-center Pineapple designs. It would make a great series.

MY PINEAPPLE QUILT

CHROMA VI: NEBULA is one of a series of Pineapple quilts in which a wash of color follows the diagonal designs in the overall pattern. I have used analogous colors in prints, as well as runs of dyed fabrics.

The quilt was prompted by a batch of sueded hand-dyed cottons from Cherrywood Fabrics with colors progressing from navy to red through purple. The dyer worked with me to get sueded red through gold for a total of 14 colors.

I piece on foundations made from computer-generated patterns printed on lightweight paper. I used colored pencils to work out the entire quilt on a design sheet. The blocks were numbered, and the design changes were written on each foundation to avoid confusion and to simplify the piecing process. I don't use templates. Instead, I precut long strips across the fabric width, so when I sew, I can just reach for the appropriate-sized strip.

I would like people who view my quilt to see the vast possibilities in the Pineapple design. It is such a versatile pattern, whether it is made in a classic traditional manner or used innovatively to create another design altogether.

I like the idea of using hand and machine quilting in the same piece. The softer line of the hand stitches juxtaposed with the hard line of machine stitches is a good design tool.

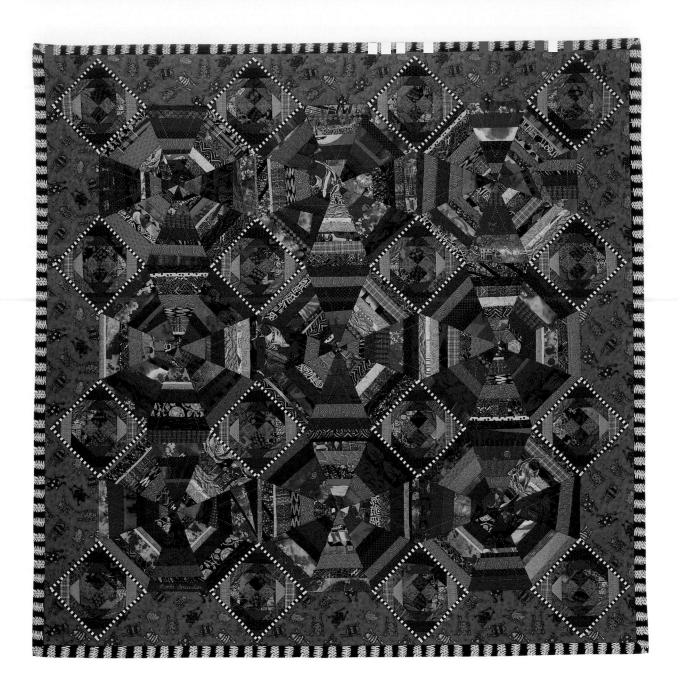

Pineapple Pie©

64" x 64", 1996
Cotton fabric and batting
Machine pieced, appliquéd, and quilted

Marta Amundson
Riverton, Wyoming

MY QUILTING

Since our ranch in Wyoming is seven cattle guards from civilization, I use my connections in the quilt world as a means to occasionally get away. Unlike my more conservative neighbors, quilters tend to embrace a liberal woman with lofty ideals about saving the animals on our planet. They think my work is important and I do, too.

Ten months of the year, I make quilts in my studio, write articles about quilting and lecture here in the States. I also find time for bird watching and fly fishing, the two activities that best indulge my passion for the outdoors. During the other two months, I travel and teach quilting in Britain, Sweden, Australia, or Brazil. I also make time to research new patterns and animals for quilts, in places like Egypt and India.

Most of my quilts were originally sparked by a deep and heartfelt feeling of injustice. Through my quilts, I try to gently nudge other people to think about what is happening in our world. Maintaining a sense of humor in my presentation helps the public more readily digest the message. I'm not what you would call a radical force, but I do have more than a few opinions, and I use my quilts as a voice to express them.

MY PINEAPPLE QUILT

Hawaii is the extinction capital of the United States, with roughly one-third of the endangered species in the entire country. In the past two centuries, approximately 40 percent of Hawaii's native bird species have become extinct. Feral pigs, goats, sheep, ants, and domestic cattle join forces with mongooses, mosquitoes, and men in taking their unfair share of the PINE-APPLE PIE.

The pie shapes were strip pieced and cut with a kaleidoscope template. I built the Pineapple blocks with 1½" strips bound with a black and white striped fabric. These blocks were carefully applied to the "holes" left when the "pies" were sewn together. Three small fish, cut from fabric, were machine appliquéd to the surface with extra batting and fusible web.

I quilted the whole quilt with mono-filament thread in a spiral pattern that radiates from the center of each pie outward. The frog fabric in the borders was heavily quilted by drawing around the frogs with a free-motion foot and making funny little loops that join the stitching lines.

Anyone with patience and a healthy scrap bag can make a quilt like PINEAPPLE PIE.

Kilauea

63¾" x 63¾", 1997
Cotton fabrics, cotton/polyester batting
Machine paper pieced and quilted

Shirley Robinson Davis
Prescott, Arizona

MY QUILTING

In 1987, while I was living on a ranch in the Ruby Mountains of northern Nevada, I was talked into taking a quilting class. I had really dragged my feet because I didn't want to get involved in another project. I had been a professional photographer, but I had put that on the back burner because I became allergic to the chemicals in my darkroom. Being snowed in much of the time out in the boondocks was making me crawl the walls, so I relented and took the class.

I guess you could say I was hooked, because after the first quilt was finished, I planned a second and a third. I started buying fabric, and it became apparent that I was going to be a quilter instead of a photographer.

I love scrap quilts because they aren't planned, they just happen. I don't have one particular style, I like to do it all. I have entered a few contests, won some prizes, and had my work juried into shows, but that's not as important to me as just sitting down and sewing a scrap quilt and totally enjoying the whole process. I have also taught a number of classes, from landscape quilts to machine appliqué and everything in between. Like I said, I love it all!

MY PINEAPPLE QUILT

KILAUEA was made especially for the 1997 MAQS contest. I designed the quilt on the computer and was able to print out the elongated blocks. I can't say enough about using the computer—no more drafting tools and graph paper and long, time-consuming drawings, only to find out it doesn't work.

I worked with the Pineapple design quite a while, and nothing seemed to work until I saw a documentary on TV about the volcano Kilauea in Hawaii. Then things started to fall in place colorwise. I decided to try to interpret the volcano with the hot lava flowing down to the sea.

I played a lot of "what if" in designing this quilt and finally hit on the idea of using three different sizes of blocks, the large ones being the volcano; and the sashing and cornerstones the lava, vegetation, and water. The set pieces represent the ocean. I would like people to try to imagine the red hot lava flowing down the mountain into the jungle and gradually turning to ash when it gets to the sea. If you look at the quilt closely, you can see four large turquoise stars in the center where the sashing and cornerstones meet.

I rarely make a final color decision on the computer, just a rough idea, because things change when you work with fabric.

Wild Pineapples

54" x 54", 1997
Cotton fabrics
Paper pieced, machine quilted,
hand and machine embroidered

Mary Esson Dowling
Grant Park, Illinois

MY QUILTING

I have been intrigued with fabric for a long time, even before I became a quiltmaker—its color, texture, design, and pattern. I had a traditional background when I started quilting 12 to 15 years ago, but I was soon taken with some of the new, artistic quilts.

Originally, I hand pieced and hand quilted. Today, I am still hand quilting, and I feel that my freestyle quilting gives my pieces a unique flavor. It usually takes me a few months to complete a piece, but I don't consider this a negative. As I become more familiar with a quilt, I find that it defines the line and movement required to give it appeal. Most of my work is colorful and often whimsical. I have a passion for gardening, and that is often reflected in some of my pieces.

Six years ago, we moved from Connecticut back to the Midwest. The first thing I did after moving was locate a guild. Although I have my parents and many old friends in my area, I knew I needed the friendship, enrichment, encouragement, and support a guild offers. I belong to Quilters Plus, which meets in Flossmoor, Illinois, and the Professional Art Quilters Alliance, which meets at the College of Du Page in Glen Ellyn, Illinois.

MY PINEAPPLE QUILT

WILD PINEAPPLES is a quilt I would never have made if it were not for the MAQS contest. I developed the quilt design on graph paper, which is how many of my pieces get their start. When I see a design in my mind's eye, the image is not always clear, and often when it is completed, it is not the same as I first imagined it. But my graph paper design is the starting point.

Quilters are often told about the importance of value, and I believe my quilt is a good example. As I made each block, I noted on my paper pattern where I would put the light fabrics, medium-lights, mediums, medium-darks, etc. The color didn't matter so much, just the value. I think fabric selection can be difficult to do because we're always striving to attain the correct color, the best fabric, to put in our pieces. There were a couple of blocks that I had to discard because the fabrics I had chosen did not show up as I thought they should.

I used Melody Johnson's hand-dyed thread for the machine embroidery. It goes through a 90/14 needle, and I used nylon thread in the bobbin. The long thread tails were hand stitched, and the ends were hidden between the layers.

> I have a great appreciation for antique fabrics, so I'll often include a piece or two wherever I can.

Leaf Fall

55" x 55", 1997
Cotton fabrics
Machine pieced, appliquéd, and quilted, and hand beaded

Gertrude S. Embree & M. Gayle Wallace
Shreveport and Taylor, Louisiana

OUR QUILTMAKING

Gertrude: I have been working in fiber forever. I like to make things. The knowledge that I can symbolize an idea, feeling, or emotion in my favorite materials is an intoxicating and powerful force. I make quilts because I like the materials. The colors and textures are seductive, and the process is something I can control.

Lately, I have been making paper collages and have created a three-dimensional piece. It is a nine-foot painted wood sculpture, incorporating quilt designs. It was commissioned by the city, and it stands on Shreveport's main street.

Gayle: Quilting entered my life in 1985. It was something I thought I would never try. But many quilts and classes later, I consider myself a quilter. When I travel, the sewing machine goes with me. This year, two quilts were finished in hotel rooms while I was on vacation.

Other quilters and students in classes that I've taught have inspired me to do more. Ideas feed off of ideas. When I see what has been done with patterns from classes, I want to do something new and exciting with the same design. Changing the design and making it "mine" is always a challenge.

OUR PINEAPPLE QUILT

Gertrude: The primary source of inspiration for LEAF FALL was a classic fall weekend on Lake Michigan. I thought perhaps my spiky design lines and color choices were suggested by the pineapple plant. My subconscious, however, was working in another direction.

After the quilt was finished and I was unsuccessfully attempting to give it a "pineapple" name, I made a surprising discovery. When I saw the photos from that weekend, I noticed that all the colors in these pictures had made their way into the quilt. The amber and golds, which I thought were pineapple slices, were leaves falling into golden carpets. The greens were grasses, plants, and trees in the woods and meadow. The silvery edges of the quilt were of course the water. Why my subconscious had kept this little secret is still a mystery, but I rather like knowing that the contents of my mental compost heap can yield a rich harvest.

Gayle: Gertrude designed and pieced the Pineapple quilt. Then for the quilting, she wanted some leaves to swirl around the outside of it, so she cut some leaves out and arranged them. I then quilted it after trying samples of different threads. When the quilting was finished, Gertrude added beading to it.

Gertrude: In trying to use the Pineapple block in a new way, I mentally set a firecracker in the center of the block and blew it apart.

29

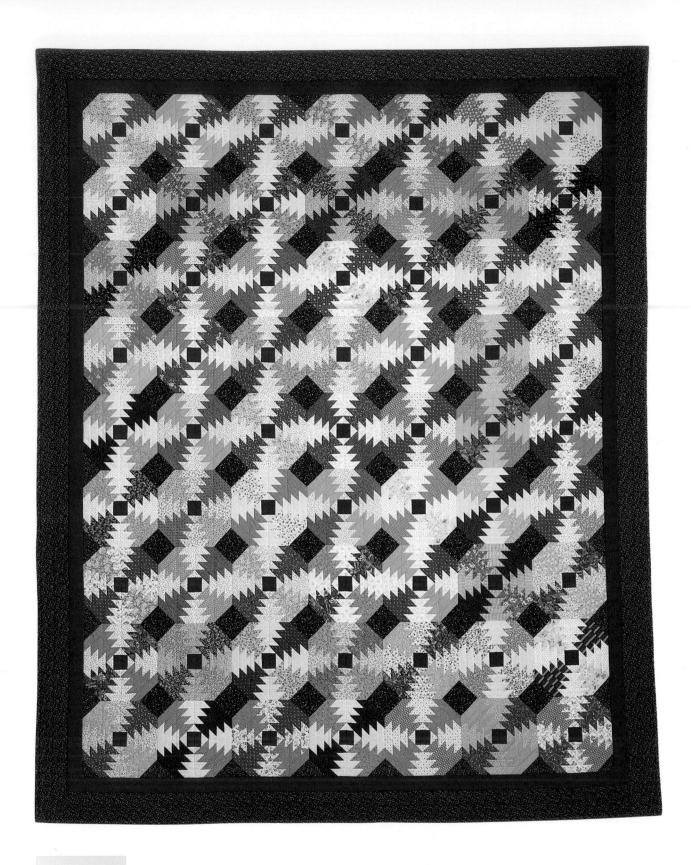

Pieceful Pineapple

82" x 100", 1993
Cotton fabrics
Paper pieced, machine quilted

Armida R. James
Ottawa, Illinois

MY QUILTING

I became interested in quilts when I was a young girl. My mother was a seamstress, and she made many comforters. Because she was a busy farm wife, she chose to tie her quilts, and I was taught at an early age to help. Later, when I became a pastor's wife, I learned to quilt under the direction of the church ladies, who quilted to earn money for the missions.

In 1982, when my four children were no longer under foot, I took my first piecing lessons and made a pillow top. Soon my ambitions drove me to make a real quilt. I chose a time-consuming pattern, sometimes called Odd Fellows. This quilt is still my only one completely hand pieced and hand quilted. It is a queen size with about 720 pieces, all of different prints, many of which were given to me by friends.

By then, my love for quilting was so strong that I bravely began making quilts for each of my 11 grandchildren. To date, I have completed nine for them and five to eventually give away.

I make quilts for the joy I find not only in creating them, but also in seeing the finished product. I enjoy showing my quilts to friends who drop by.

MY PINEAPPLE QUILT

At a class on paper-piecing Pineapple quilts, my teacher inspired me to make PIECEFUL PINEAPPLE. It has 63 blocks with 37 pieces in each block, making a total of 2,331 pieces.

Paper piecing was new to me, but I thoroughly enjoyed making this quilt. I tried to place the emphasis on choosing colors to complement each other within each block. It was interesting trying out different combinations from my fabric collection.

Eventually, when this quilt was completed, I showed it to my teacher, and she gave me the courage to enter the MAQS contest.

Had I thought, in my wildest dreams, that my quilt would be chosen as a finalist, I wonder if I would have done something differently. Would the quilt be more exotic if I had spent more time arranging blocks? Perhaps I should have thought seriously about a colorwash affect. When I mentioned these thoughts to a seasoned quilter, she reminded me that perhaps my quilt would not have been chosen had it been any different from the random way it is arranged.

> If I make another Pineapple quilt, I think paper piecing would still be my choice. It is nice to have blocks come out the same size.

Broken Arrow

55½" x 56", 1997
Cotton fabrics, wool batting
Paper pieced, machine quilted

FINALIST

Linda Juniér
Sedona, Arizona

MY QUILTING

I really enjoy quilt challenges. They exercise my brain and stimulate my creative juices. My thinking usually starts with "I wonder what would happen if..." and leads me in all kinds of directions.

I began quilting in 1994 after moving to Sedona, Arizona, and have been obsessed and consumed ever since. It seems to be a familiar history among quilters, sewing doll clothes as a child and developing a life-long love affair with color and fabric. Moving from clothing design and construction to quilting was a natural evolution for me.

The people who influenced me initially were the Amish. I admire their work ethic and how they focus completely on the work at hand. I've also been influenced by everyone I've taken a class from. You can always learn something, little tips, small insights, and even big ah-ha's.

I have lived in spectacular Sedona since 1994 with my husband, Ron. Living among the beautiful red rocks is inspirational. Creativity flows easily and naturally when surrounded by such a picturesque landscape.

Currently, I am working on a series of larger-than-life floral quilts inspired by the paintings of Georgia O'Keeffe. It's a new way of working for me, using large and bold areas of flowing color.

MY PINEAPPLE QUILT

I used a computer program to stretch the traditional square Pineapple quilt block into a rectangle. I then decided on the size of the rectangle and drafted a paper-piecing pattern, so I could accurately execute the new block.

Black and white fabrics are always so visually powerful. Stripes create interesting effects and surprises. By combining both, I felt I would achieve maximum impact. My homage to tradition was to use red centers, albeit plaid.

I used triangles as the first border to reinforce the feeling of angles in the Pineapple blocks. The second border was a narrow red band. The final one was a three-triangle-square border that I have used before with striped fabrics. That idea came from a magazine article by Mary Mashuta. It wasn't until the quilt was completed that I realized that the piece had a Southwestern feeling, hence the name BROKEN ARROW.

Fellow quilters should be aware of the use of stripes in Pineapple quilts and how much fun they are to work with!

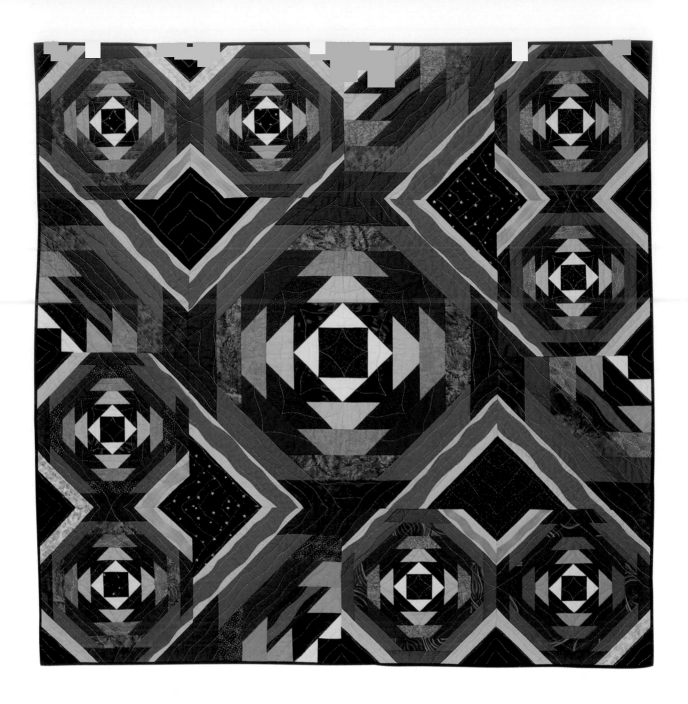

Pineapple Strata
60" x 60", 1997
Commercial and hand-dyed cottons
Machine foundation pieced and quilted

Patricia Klem
Rancho Santa Fe, California

MY QUILTING

I began quilting about 20 years ago when my children were small. They learned from the beginning to respect mom's tools, to step over my blocks on the floor, and to walk with a slight shuffle to avoid any pins hiding in the carpet.

In addition to majoring in textiles and clothing design in college, I took many quilting classes, beginning with Jean Ray Laury in 1977, to learn as many techniques as possible. Since then, I have studied with many wonderful quilt artists. In addition, I have been inspired for color and design by the works of masters like van Gogh and Cézanne and some contemporary artists.

One of the highlights of my quilting life was being asked by the Monterey Diocese to design and supervise construction of a quilt to be given to the Pope when he visited California in 1987. I was able to meet with and present this gift to John Paul II.

I love to travel, recently bringing back a suitcase full of fabric from Pakistan. My husband and I have joined a home exchange program, so who knows where that will take us.

MY PINEAPPLE QUILT

I surprised even myself when I decided to undertake the precision of a Pineapple quilt. In designing, I often used the computer or the copy machine to experiment with combining different sizes of blocks or shapes.

I wanted to have a design with depth and movement, so I began with a 4" Pineapple block and enlarged it to 15". Then I enlarged the 15" block to 30" and made several copies of each. The larger block was cut into quarters to match the measurement of the smaller block. I then experimented with various arrangements until I decided on the one for PINEAPPLE STRATA. In the future, I would like to try this method with other traditional blocks to see what would result.

Commercial cottons in gradated colors were used to create a sense of movement. I drew the paper patterns for foundation piecing but couldn't resist adding accents of curved piecing and curved, freeform machine quilting.

The color combinations in this quilt were inspired by *Roche-Taille*, a painting by French abstractionist Jean Bazaine.

Bits and Bytes

58" x 58", 1997

Cotton fabrics, soutache braid, and pony beads

Paper pieced, hand quilted

Lois Monieson
Kingston, Ontario, Canada

MY QUILTING

I especially like to work with plaids and have made plaid quilts from the Kaleidoscope, Monkey Wrench, uneven Log Cabin, and quarter-square triangle patterns.

I like to make quilts in which the pattern, design, and color carry across many blocks. No two blocks have the same coloration in BITS AND BYTES, and none of the blocks are interchangeable. I enjoy this type of challenge. Working this way requires a vertical design wall, which I made out of two 4' x 8', 2"-thick styrofoam insulation sheets on which I glued pellon fleece.

This is the first time I've made a Pineapple quilt. I've made five Log Cabin quilts (a sister to the Pineapple quilt), including BUTTER-FLIES ARE FREE, which was a finalist in the 1995 MAQS contest. The next time I make a Pineapple quilt, I would like to try an off-center design. I find myself increasingly moving toward art quilts.

MY PINEAPPLE QUILT

BITS AND BYTES was machine sewn on vellum foundation blocks. It has 4,500 pieces (bits) in 131 different fabrics (bytes) and contains embellishments to simulate computer chip connections.

I designed my quilt layout by using a grid found in a pattern book. I colored the design with markers and made a master layout by drawing a grid with tailor's chalk on my design wall. I numbered each block, then cut all the fabrics into the strips needed. The strips for each block were pinned together and arranged in bundles on the master layout until I was satisfied with their placement. I assigned numbers to the strips and entered the numbers on the master layout. Because of the complexity of BITS AND BYTES, I carefully followed my master layout.

Before starting to piece, I marked the division lines for each fabric used on the paper foundations. In addition, on the back of the paper foundation, I marked the number of each block according to the master layout along with a directional arrow. As the blocks were sewn, they were returned to their place on the master layout.

> To me, the quilt suggests the frenetic nature of society today in which we all seem to be connected in this complex technological world.

Anne's Pineapple Plantation: How Did the Nine Patches Get in There?

63" x 50", 1996
Cotton fabrics
Paper pieced, hand quilted

Anne J. Oliver
Alexandria, Virginia

MY QUILTING

While looking at a quilt show in California in the mid-1970s, I felt I could create quilts better than some I had seen, even though I had never made one. After tackling a Dresden Plate with no instruction, I found I was wrong. I still managed to finish my first quilt, even with all its mistakes.

After being disappointed with oils, watercolors, etc., I found I could express myself nicely in quilting. It was not as exacting as other art forms, yet the final piece of work was large, impressive, and creative.

My next project will probably be a continuation of taking an old pattern and carrying it a step further. Perhaps I'll try another Dresden Plate, but this time the quality will be vastly improved, and I will not be quilting three stitches to the inch. Though I've never counted my stitches, I do know I can do better than the "saddle-stitching" I did on my first quilt.

MY PINEAPPLE QUILT

To make PINEAPPLE PLAN-TATION, I cut paper-piecing Pineapple patterns into fourths. Using 1" finished strips, I machine stitched each section. Then a 1" strip was added to the pattern so that a Nine Patch resulted. I wanted the quilt to look like ripe pineapples in a field, surrounded by palm trees.

The palm fronds were separately sewn and stuffed, then stitched to the completed quilt. I wasn't sure the idea would work. I have a habit of not sketching my ideas on paper. It gets me in trouble at times, but for some reason, for me, a sketched idea is changed so many times before I execute it, that it's easier to take chances and move ideas around until they look right. I do not recommend my method for most quilters.

I've competed in many shows, partly because they made me finish my work.

Focus I

64" x 78½", 1997
Cottons and cotton blends
Machine and hand pieced and hand quilted

Elizabeth Rymer
Hurricane Mills, Tennessee

MY QUILTING

The Pineapple pattern has a special meaning for me, because this pattern is where quilting began in my life. In 1975, I was walking through a bookstore when a small magazine on quilting caught my eye. As I looked at the quilts, an Amish Pineapple quilt caught my attention, and for the first time, I thought of making a quilt. I bought the magazine and decided to give the Pineapple a try. With only a 2" line drawing and few instructions to work from, this quilt proved to be quite a challenge. After many failed attempts, I managed a pattern and, after many months, I had a 36" square put together. Even though it was far from perfect, I was totally hooked.

For the last 20 years, we have lived in small towns, and I have been a lone quilter. All has been learned from trial and error, books and magazines. A great deal of my time is spent experimenting and trying new ideas on small swatches.

To be happy, I must be creating, and quilting fills this need for me in a way that knitting, weaving, painting, and other things have never come close to. With quilts, there is never an end to what can be created.

MY PINEAPPLE QUILT

When I began planning my Pineapple quilt for this contest, I was in the mood for bright colors. My first idea for the center section was to have the Pineapple pattern in each puzzle piece. After completing several of these and placing them together, I felt it was too busy and needed something for separation. I decided on something simple that would not compete with the busy Pineapple sections. The black and white seemed to bring it all together.

In the beginning, I thought only of the center section. I needed to complete it before I could proceed to work outward. This was a different approach for me because I usually plan the complete design on paper first. I randomly dyed white cotton with several shades of gray to get the effect I was after for the outer sections. In a small town with just one source for fabric, you are limited as to selection. More and more, I use dye in some way to develop an interesting fabric.

I used curves in my quilting to keep the feeling of motion. My method of quilting freely has a bonus because you don't have any marks to remove. I enjoy the freedom to be spontaneous and break all the rules.

I began quilting FOCUS I with no plan in mind, feeling free to go in any direction as the mood hit.

Pineapple-R-Squared
60" x 60", 1997
Cotton fabric and batting
Machine pieced and quilted, fused appliqué

Ida M. Tendam
West Lafayette, Indiana

MY QUILTING

My quilting interest began in 1985, when I took my first quilting class at a local fabric store. I sometimes feel, that, if I would just devote my efforts to one specialization, I would be able to make the perfect quilt. The problem is, I like all areas of quilting. Just when I think I'm able to focus on one aspect, a terrific workshop will be offered somewhere. Then I'm off and running in another direction.

In my real life, I am an administrative assistant in the Division of Interdisciplinary Engineering Studies at Purdue University. In this capacity, I counsel students toward their academic pursuits and manage the office. Quilting provides the creative outlet I need so that I can face each day fresh and interested in that new student who asks the same questions I've already heard several times.

I make quilts to make me whole, but more than that, I believe that quilting provides the tactile experience that I can get nowhere else. From early childhood, we are admonished "don't touch." With quilting, touching is everything, from that bolt of fabric in the fabric store that I hug and pet on its way to the cutting counter, to that final finished quilt that touches both the heart and hand. If you're a quilter, it's not only okay to touch, it's required.

MY PINEAPPLE QUILT

PINEAPPLE-R-SQUARED was started in a class on foundation piecing. I had just enough hand-dyed fabric to do four blocks. This project was set aside for a couple of years. When I got back to it, I saw it with new eyes, partly because of the MAQS competition.

I used two sizes of commercial paper-piecing foundations, a 4" and a 12" Pineapple block. After piecing the 4" block, I placed it in the center of the larger block foundation and continued piecing until the 12" block was finished.

I knew I wanted to set the four blocks on point and use them as a medallion surrounded by some kind of appliqué. I considered the traditional Hawaiian appliqué Pineapple. The original pattern was for a square, but I played with just a half-square triangle. I purchased some additional fabric, which I now feel enhances the medallion more than if I'd had enough of the hand-dyed fabric to finish the quilt. I fused the appliqués to my quilt rather than hand stitching them. Then I satin stitched around them.

I used echo quilting for this piece, with just a touch of stippling in some areas. I like echo quilting because the top doesn't need to be marked first.

> Sometimes, in the process of finishing an old project, I get a new idea. That's exactly what happened with PINEAPPLE-R-SQUARED.

Hidden Pineapples

72" x 84", 1996
Cotton fabrics and cotton/polyester batting
Paper pieced, hand quilted

Joan Will
Bend, Oregon

MY QUILTING

More than 30 years ago, my mother-in-law gave me some hand-pieced quilt blocks made by her mother and sister in the early 1900s. There were six different patterns for six quilts. I knew nothing about quilting, and I was not particularly interested.

In the 1980s, my sister opened her own quilt-fabric shop and inspired me some, but I was working and really didn't have the time. After I retired, I wanted to assemble and finish the blocks my mother-in-law had given me, especially because I felt they were heirlooms and they should be passed on to my children someday.

I completed three of the tops before I took a class, and I am not particularly proud of them. They were definitely learning experiences. Then I signed up for a class, and the instructor was a wonderful inspiration to all of us. I completed the quilt I had taken to the class and started on others.

I'm hooked. I find hand quilting very relaxing, and I can do it while watching TV. My interest in quilting also gives me the opportunity to volunteer at our local museum as part of a Homestead Skills interpretation.

MY PINEAPPLE QUILT

I took a class in paper piecing. One of the samples the instructor had was a two-color block. I was impressed and went home and started making a two-color block in blue and white. It was okay, but it looked dead to me. When I viewed my sample in a mirror, angled at 45 degrees, and laid various scraps on the top, I discovered the pattern I then used in HIDDEN PINEAPPLES.

In the quilt, the black triangles create a circular pattern throughout. I was happy with the result and wanted to keep going. There are 48 6" blocks in the center. To enlarge the top to a size that would be useful, I added several borders.

I am satisfied with the design I accomplished. If I were to make it again, I would experiment with the orientation of the blocks and use a different color selection just for variation.

My choice of the white-on-white 8" border was specifically planned because I wanted to learn how to draft and quilt the feather pattern.

Sliced Pineapple

56" x 84", 1997
Cottons, silks, photo transfers
Machine pieced and quilted

Adrienne Yorinks
North Salem, New York

MY QUILTING

I was born on Staten Island, New York, but I now live in North Salem, New York, with my husband, Arthur, and our five dogs: three border collies and two red poodles.

I am a fabric artist, who likes to blend the traditional and the modern. I received two significant commissions. The City University of New York asked me to create a piece of art to commemorate their 150th anniversary. Using rarely seen archival photos and documents from the university's library, I created an 8½' x 10', nine-panel work tracing the university's history. The piece, entitled "Look at Their Faces," will be on tour in New York City until 1999.

In addition, I was commissioned to illustrate Marian Wright Edelman's upcoming book, *Stand for Children* (Hyperion Books, 1998). Marian is the founder and director of The Children's Defense Fund in Washington, D.C., and this coming year marks their 25th anniversary. For the book, I created 26 quilts to illustrate Marian's moving text. All 26 works will tour the United States, starting in 1998.

MY PINEAPPLE QUILT

My first Pineapple quilt was quite traditional. It was a commission for the noted artist Maurice Sendak. He is an avid collector of early Disney objects, and he had numerous pieces of Disney fabric from 1930, which he didn't know how to display. They made a wonderful Pineapple quilt.

For SLICED PINEAPPLE, I asked myself, what are the components of the traditional Pineapple block, what are the components of the pineapple fruit, why is a pineapple so pleasing and comforting, so much so that it became a symbol of comfort in furniture and of hospitality in shops. I dissected the block and began restructuring it in my mind.

A pineapple doesn't quite sit straight; it is slightly askew. I wanted to create a link between the fruit, at once tangy and sweet, to the softness of the fabric and the angular cut pieces. I saw an opportunity to incorporate all three of my working styles: photo transfers, abstract expressionism, and a kind of revisionism of the traditional pattern. I used fabrics that are familiar to me: cotton, silk, vintage and hand-dyed fabrics, along with some photo transfers of canned pineapple labels.

> I used a color palette that evoked both the inside and the outside of the fruit all at once.

Pineapple Patterns
Block Patterns

Included in this section are full-size templates for traditional Pineapple blocks in six sizes. Select the size most appropriate for your fabrics and project plans. You will also find some Pineapple quilt design ideas to jump start your imagination. (For foundation piecing instructions see Jane Hall's "Foundation Piecing" on page 92.)

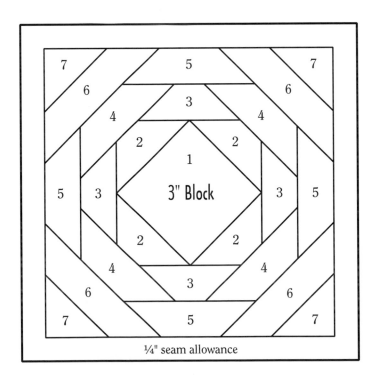

¼" seam allowance

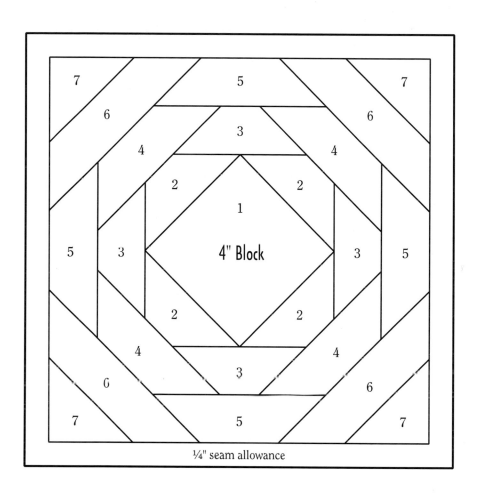

7   5   7

6   6

3

4   4

2   2

1

4" Block

5   3   3   5

2   2

4   4

3

6   6

7   5   7

¼" seam allowance

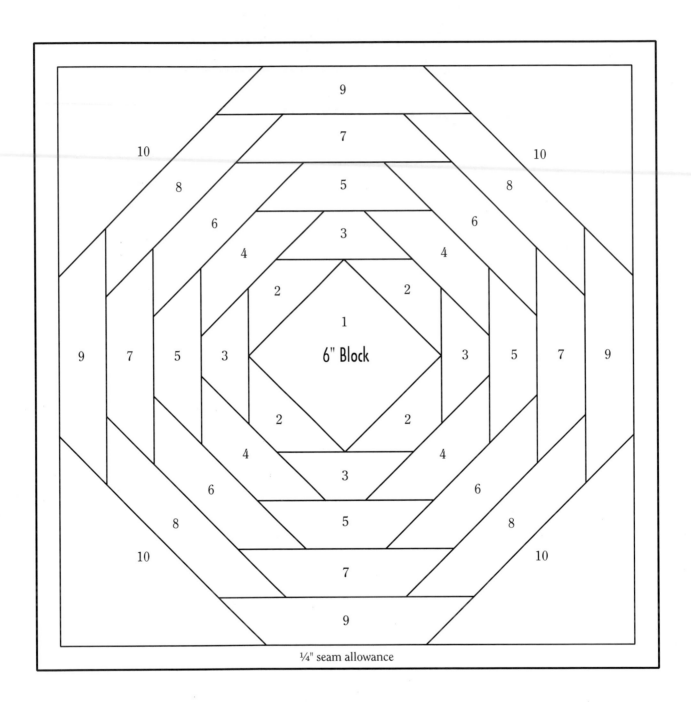

¼" seam allowance

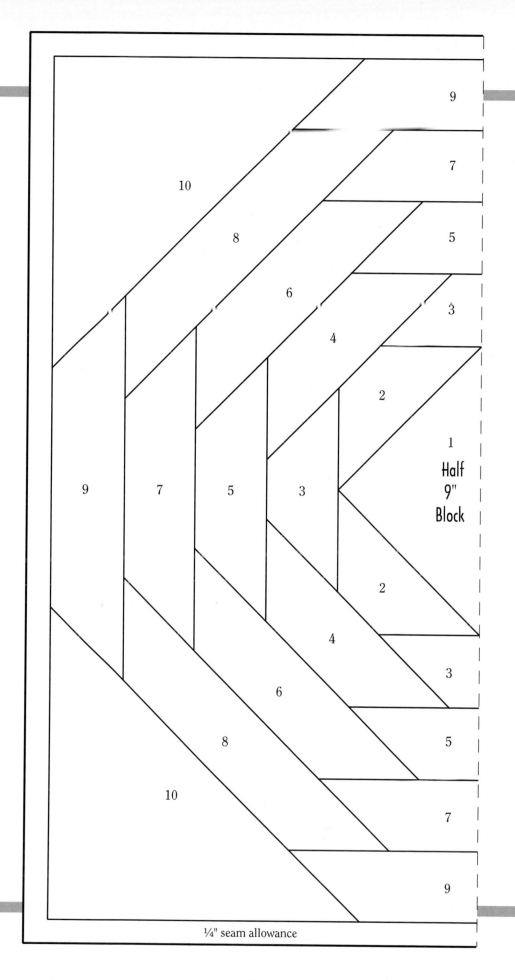

Half
9"
Block

¼" seam allowance

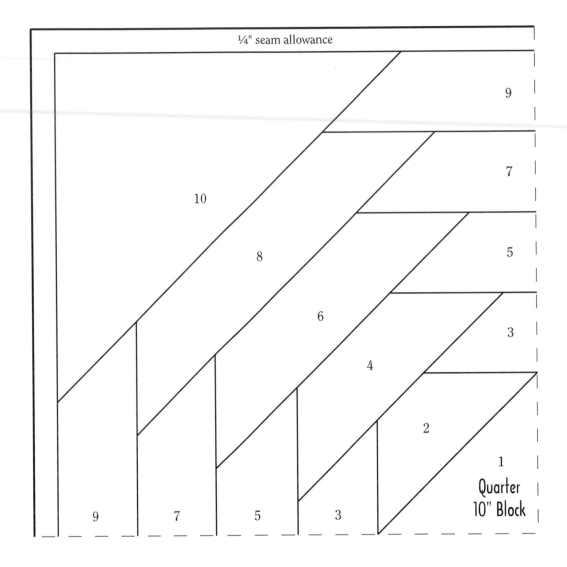

¼" seam allowance

9

7

5

3

1

Quarter
10" Block

10

8

6

4

2

9   7   5   3

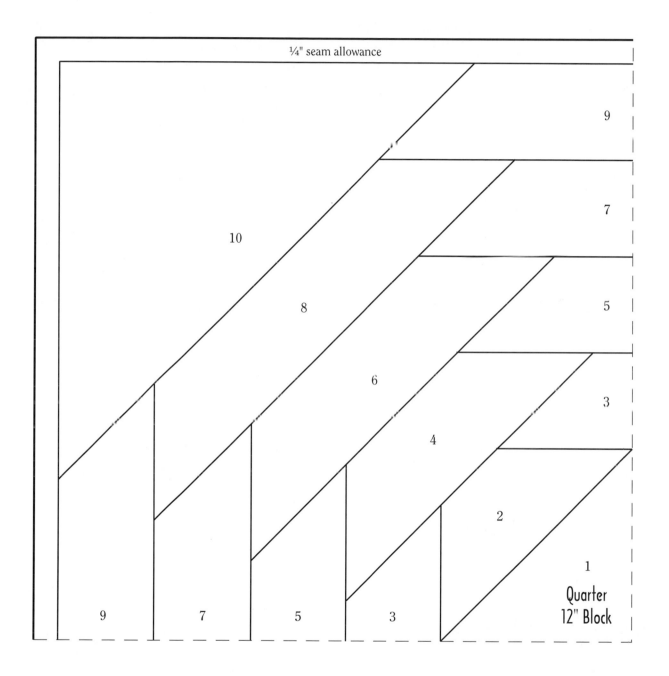

¼" seam allowance

9

7

5

3

1

Quarter
12" Block

10

8

6

4

2

9

7

5

3

Quilt Designs

Quilt Designs

Quilt Designs

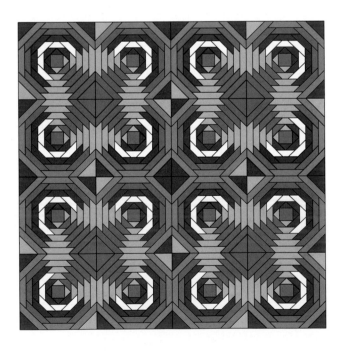

Working with the Design
Tips & Techniques

PAINTED PINEAPPLE, detail, by Mary Ann Herndon. Full quilt shown on page 12.

Off-Center Pineapples
by Mary Ann Herndon

Mary Ann Herndon designed this playful off-center Pineapple block for her quilt PAINTED PINEAPPLE, page 12. She used a 10" block for her quilt, and you will probably want to enlarge this 5" paper-foundation pattern for your project. (Be sure to use a digital photocopier, so the blocks will not be distorted.)

Enlarge	Finished Size
140%	7"
180%	9"
200%	10"

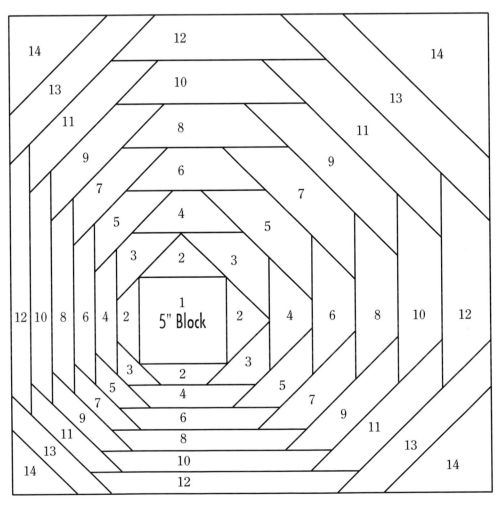

Mary's off-center Pineapple block, half size. After enlarging, add ¼" seam allowances.

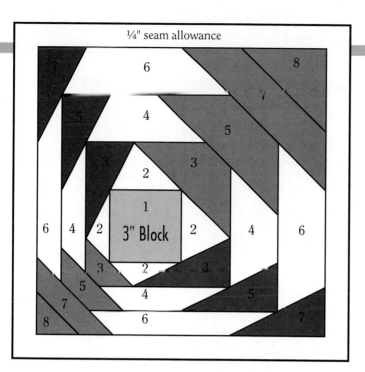

Off-Center Pineapples
by Joan Will

Joan Will used 6" off-center blocks for her quilt HIDDEN PINEAPPLES, page 44 and 60. Here is her block, presented in 3" and 5" sizes.

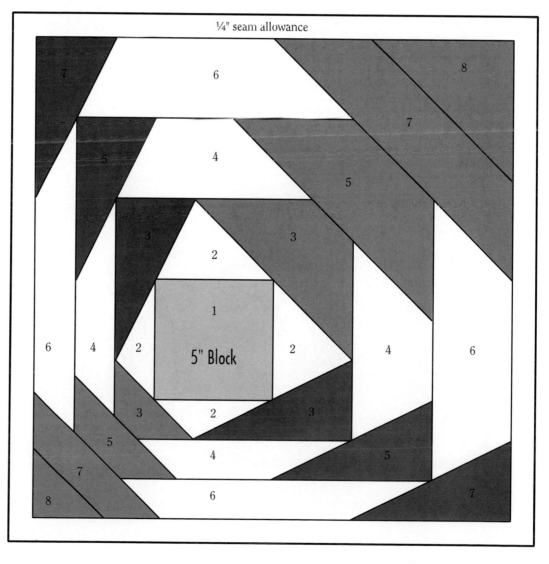

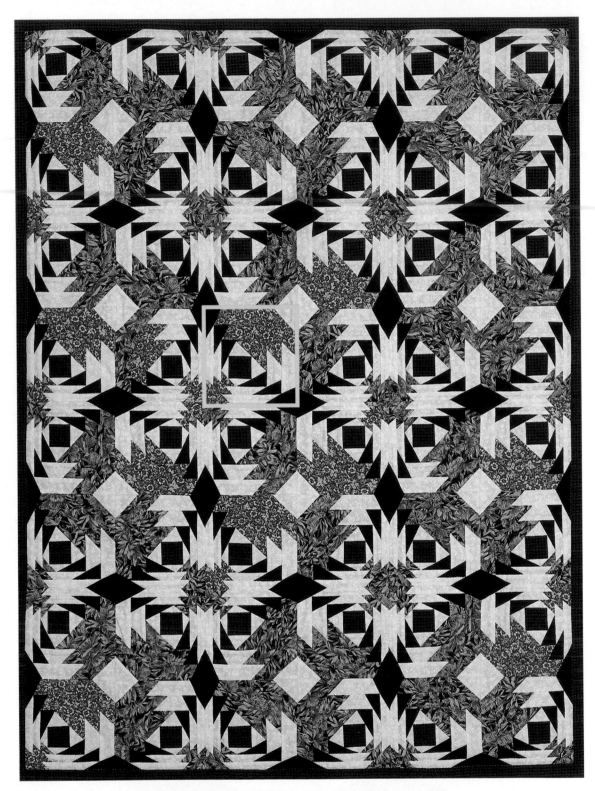

HIDDEN PINEAPPLES, detail, 72" x 84", 1996, by Joan Will.
One block is highlighted so you can see how the coloration of
the off-center block creates the circular pattern. Full quilt is
shown on page 44.

Designing Pineapple Pie
by Marta Amundson

As with most of my quilts, PINEAPPLE PIE started as a verbal idea. I then tried to make my fabric speak a visual language that would invite a viewer to ask questions. With a double-split complementary color concept in mind, I went to my scrap basket and pulled out three color families: yellow, fuchsia, and turquoise.

Strip piecing in a random fashion, I made my fabric, which was then cut with a Kaleidoscope template to form the wedges of the pie. I used my design wall to lay out the wedges. After the blocks were sewn together, it was apparent what size Pineapple blocks would be needed to fill the spaces between the Nine Patch of pies.

I cut and pieced the Pineapple blocks and bound the edges with a black-and-white striped fabric. This frame visually separated the elements, so that the overall pattern was not lost in a brilliance of hot color. Likewise, I repeated the black-and-white motif in the binding to stabilize the overkill of vibrant colors.

The Pineapple blocks were ¼" to ⅜" larger all around than the "holes." A glue stick held the blocks in place over the openings while I top stitched them about a needle's width in from the edges.

It was not accidental that small amounts of turquoise fabric turned up in the blocks and wedges. This complementary color, in small amounts, made the yellow and fuchsia areas even more vibrant and, at the same time, helped to integrate the border fabric so that it did not appear to be an afterthought. The small tropical fish were appliquéd to add another layer of interest to the work.

The back of the quilt included a piece of fabric that my husband had brought me from Hawaii. I wrote the quilt statement on my computer and, using freezer paper to stabilize the fabric, I sent it through the laser printer to make a large label.

PINEAPPLE PIE, detail, 64" x 64", 1996, by Marta Amundson. Full quilt is shown on page 22.

61

Make fabric from strips and use this wedge pattern to make your own PINEAPPLE PIE, or purchase a 45° wedge ruler from your local quilt shop or mail-order supplier.

place on fold

Half of
45° Wedge

Designing Leaf Fall
by Gertrude S. Embree

I started by drawing my design for LEAF FALL, pages 28 and 64, on graph paper. If you suspect that I broke up some shapes for easier sewing, you are right. I do not like inset seams. Even so, there were partial seams and flapping ends all over the place until I could sew all the sections together.

You can use photocopies of the quilt design and some colored pencils or markers to play with color and value placement. Adding or subtracting lines is allowed. Use correction fluid to block out lines you don't want and use an ultra-fine pen to add design lines or indicate seam lines. Go wild. It's your quilt.

When you are pleased with your color choices, draw a grid over the surface of the copy, using existing vertical and horizontal seam lines from the edges of the quilt. Photocopy your design with the drawn grid in place so you can have several copies to note dimensions, extra seam lines, and sewing order. Please note that the small red triangles on my quilt were appliquéd. Therefore, the color placement diagram shows the color of the strips under the appliqués (Fig. 2, page 65).

Once you have drawn the grid, decide how big you want the quilt to be. Then figure the dimensions an individual grid square will represent. For example, if there are 44 squares across the quilt and each grid square represents 1", the quilt will be 44". If each square represents 1½", the quilt will be 66".

To determine the finished size of a particular patch, multiply the number of grid squares in the width of the patch by the size you have chosen for the grid square. Repeat for the length of the patch.

To find the cut width of a patch, add ½" to the finished width for seam allowances. To determine the cut length, add a ¼" allowance to both ends of the patch if the ends are square. A patch that ends in a 45° angle requires a ⅝" seam allowance on that end and a ¼" allowance on the square end, for a total of ⅞". A patch

with 45° angles at both ends requires ⅝" added on each end, or a total of 1¼" (Fig. 1).

If one square of your graph paper equals 1", then it will be relatively easy to figure the cutting dimensions as you go; however, if one square equals something else, 1¼" for example, then it may be helpful to make a cutting chart. The chart can be as simple as assigning a letter to each patch of a given size and shape and listing the patches on a piece of paper with their cut sizes.

Pin the fabric patches to your design wall as you cut them and assess how well the color and value choices are working before you sew. Replace what displeases you.

The sewing is not difficult, but it is complicated, so go slowly. I started in the lower right corner and sewed logical sections; that is, strips that were lying in the same direction horizontally or that could be easily joined to vertical strips. When the layout prevents sewing complete seams, sew partial seams.

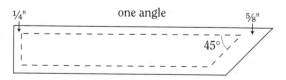

Add ½" in width; ½" in length.

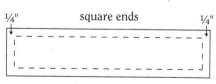

Add ½" in width; ⅞" in length.

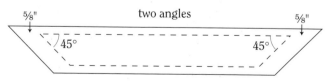

Add ½" in width; 1¼" in length.

Fig. 1. Adding seam allowances.

LEAF FALL, 55" x 55", 1997, by Gertrude S. Embree and M. Gayle Wallace.

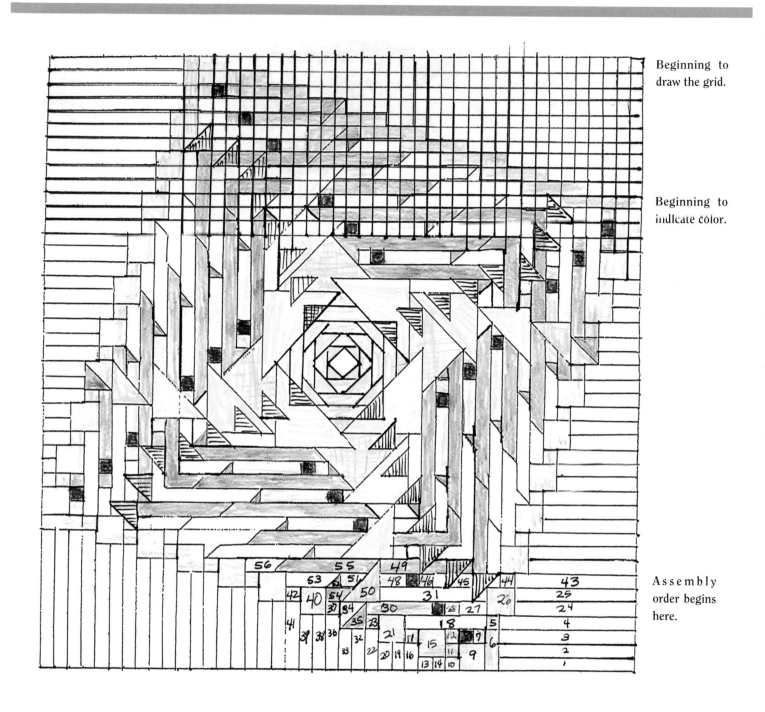

Beginning to draw the grid.

Beginning to indicate color.

Assembly order begins here.

Fig. 2. Gertrude's diagram of LEAF FALL with partial grid drawn at the top. Numbering for patch assembly order has been started in the lower right corner.

Designing Leaf Fall, Gertrude S. Embree

Fig. 3. Here is a drawing of LEAF FALL for you to enlarge and color.

From Rough Sketch to Finished Quilt
by Sherri Bain Driver

Parts of PINEAPPLE SALSA, pages 18 and 68, were drafted to fit particular sizes of motifs and widths of stripes, but I began with a rough plan of the design. I don't work out all the little details until I'm in the sewing phase. This method provides me with surprises along the way and keeps me interested enough to finish the project.

For the plan, I drew a quick sketch of the quilt on graph paper (Fig. 1). The purpose of this drawing was to get a rough idea of how the quilt would look, that is, to see if the proportions were pleasing and if the border idea complemented the central design. Because the Pineapple blocks were to be used in a fairly traditional way, I didn't draw the individual logs, but substituted Kaleidoscope blocks instead. I just needed to see with my eyes the idea I had in my mind. The second reason for the drawing was to plan the construction. Dotted lines were added to indicate major construction seams.

Next, the Pineapple block was drafted full size with a 2" square in the center to fit a motif in one of my fabrics and an 8" diagonal line in each corner to accommodate ikat stars I had made several years before. The outside logs of the block were drawn the width of another stripe that formed a subtle inner border when sewn to two outside edges of each block.

I knew I wanted to paper piece the Pineapple blocks, so I needed several copies of the block. I made 16 photocopies of a quarter of the block, trimmed each photocopy, and reconstructed the block pattern by zigzag stitching the papers together. Blocks were sewn with the flip-and-sew method of paper piecing. After the blocks were sewn together, the center star was set in.

To design the border, I made a full-sized drawing of the edge of the 19" Pineapple block on graph paper. Following my rough drawing, I extended the perpendicular lines from the blocks into the border. I measured the width of the stripes for the zigzags and drew them on the graph paper. Templates were made for all these pieces. I like to use clear plastic templates so that I can position the fabric design for each piece. I was pleasantly surprised by the border. In my rough drawing, the zigzags were all the same depth, but the quilt ended up having both deep and shallow ones.

Starting with just a rough drawing will always give you a few surprises along the way. May most of your surprises be happy ones!

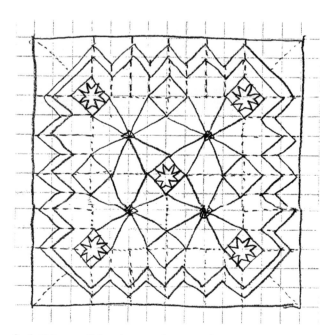

Fig. 1. This pencil drawing was the start of PINEAPPLE SALSA.

PINEAPPLE SALSA, 64" x 64", 1997, by Sherri Bain Driver.

Fig. 2. Sherri's colored pencil drawing of PINEAPPLE SALSA.

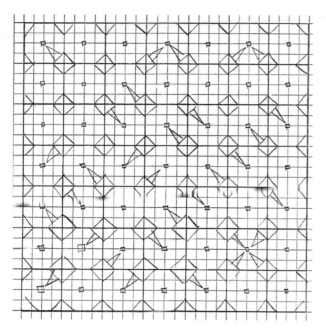

Fig. 1. Like many quilters, Mary started with a graph-paper drawing for her quilt.

Designing Wild Pineapples
by Mary Esson Dowling

The quilt design for WILD PINEAPPLES, shown below and on page 26, was developed on graph paper, and then, through the use of a wide range of color, the quilt was brought to life. This quilt was fun and exciting to do, because I had no idea if it would turn out in a way that I would like.

In planning your color placement, remember that paper-foundation piecing, with the fabric under the paper, produces a reversed image. A full-size piecing pattern appears on page 70.

WILD PINEAPPLES, 54" x 54", 1997, by Mary Esson Dowling.

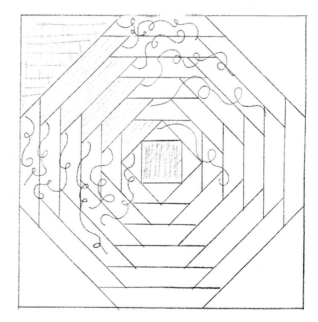

Fig. 2. Mary's drawing for WILD PINEAPPLES' machine quilting. Hand-dyed thread was used with a 90/14 needle.

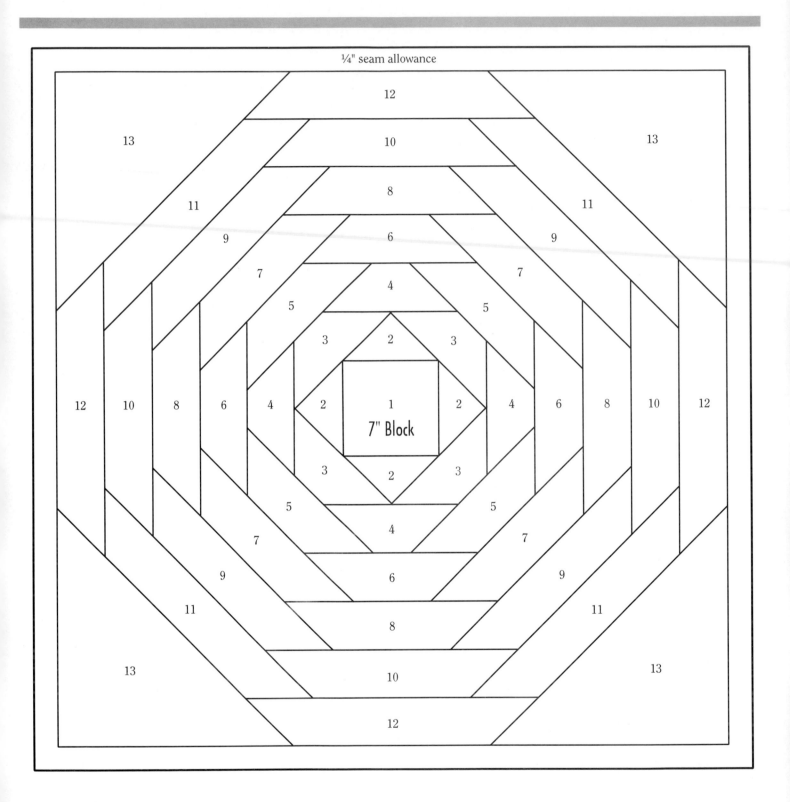

¼" seam allowance

7" Block

Mary's WILD PINEAPPLES block pattern.

Making a Puzzle Quilt
by Elizabeth Rymer

FOCUS I, 64" x 78½", 1997, by Elizabeth Rymer.

The puzzle idea I used for Focus I, page 40, has many design possibilities. You can enjoy making your own Pineapple puzzle, or you may want to try your hand at using this technique with other blocks.

The following directions assume that you will be paper piecing by sewing on the line with the fabric under the paper, rather than using the flip-and-sew method with the fabric on top.

It is important to identify each puzzle piece individually and on the master drawing. Add marks for matching the curves to the puzzle pieces to aid in sewing them together. Place a mark at each corner of the puzzle shapes where the seam lines cross, as added insurance during assembly.

PUZZLE INSTRUCTIONS
• To make your own puzzle quilt, first make a full-sized master drawing on plain newsprint or any sufficiently large sheet of paper (or sheets of paper taped together if needed).

71

- Use a flexible curve (available at art-supply stores) to draw the puzzle shapes. It's a good idea to keep the shapes large and simple, with one or two gentle curves per side of each puzzle piece. Indicate on the master drawing which puzzle pieces will become Pineapple blocks.

- To make a paper-piecing pattern for the Pineapples, trace the outline of a puzzle shape from the master drawing onto freezer paper, shiny side up. A permanent pen will work on the slick surface. You will also need a drawing of a square Pineapple block. I used a 10"-square block for Focus I. Place the square block under the

freezer-paper tracing, matte side up. You can position the center of the block anywhere within the puzzle shape. Trace the center square and the logs onto the freezer paper. Then fill in the rest of the puzzle shape with additional logs as needed (Fig. 1). You can press logs to the freezer-paper pattern as you sew.

- Paper piece the Pineapple block as usual, and trim the edges of the fabric strips to match the edges of the puzzle piece (including block seam allowances). As you complete each Pineapple puzzle piece, remove the paper and return the piece to its position on the master drawing.

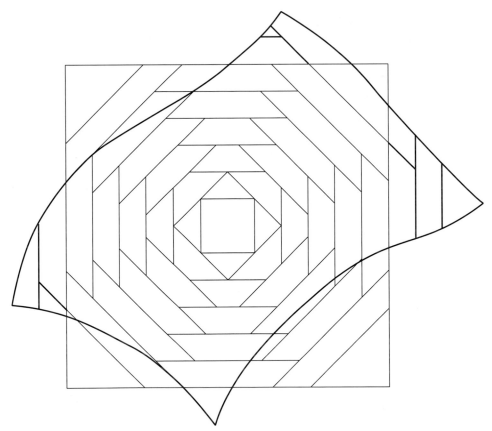

Fig.1. Place the square block under the freezer-paper tracing of the puzzle shape. Trace the logs onto the puzzle shape. Move the shape as necessary and continue tracing until the logs fill the shape.

• If you want to add black-and-white checkerboard puzzle pieces like those in Focus I, trace the shape of one of the puzzle pieces on freezer paper, shiny side up, to make a template. Include the inside lines (Fig. 2). Identify templates on the matte side so you can read the information as you work. I recommend identifying the placement of the black-and-white puzzle pieces on the master drawing to avoid cutting mistakes.

• Cut the freezer-paper templates apart. Press them onto the wrong side of the appropriate fabrics, leaving room between them for seam allowances.

• Cut the fabric patches out, adding ¼" seam allowances by eye. Sew all the patches together for the puzzle shape. To help you when it's time to sew all the puzzle shapes together, use a water-soluble pen to mark the seam lines along the paper templates on the outside edges of the shape. Repeat for each puzzle piece.

• Remove the paper and pin the puzzle pieces in place on the master drawing as you finish each one.

• Sew the puzzle pieces together in rows; then sew the rows together to complete the body of your quilt.

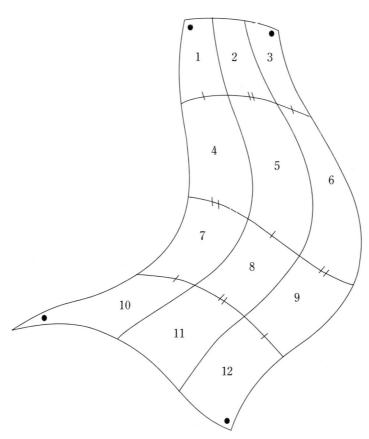

Fig. 2. Example of freezer-paper template for black-and-white checkerboard puzzle pieces.

Making a Puzzle Quilt, Elizabeth Rymer

Hawaiian Appliqué
by Ida M. Tendam

Here is a pattern similar to the one I used for the appliqué in PINEAPPLE-R-SQUARED, pictured below and on page 42. Because I was using only a diagonally cut half square, I had to improvise the folding.

The directions at right show how to fold the fabric. The appliqué fabric was first treated with a fusible material, then folded exactly as the background fabric. Once the appliqué was cut, the folds lined up perfectly for placing the appliqué on the background. Then I fused the two together.

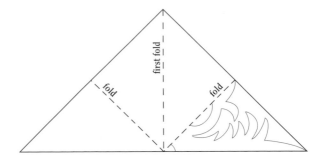

Fig. 1. Fold fabric in half on the first fold and press the fold.

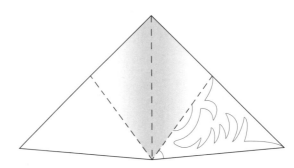

Fig. 2. Fold back one side and then the other. Press the folds.

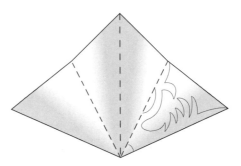

Fig. 3. Be sure to fold the sides separately so the cutting will be more accurate.

PINEAPPLE-R-SQUARED, 60" x 60", 1997, by Ida M. Tendam.

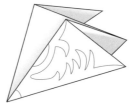

Fig. 4. Your folded fabric should look like this.

fold

Triangle Hawaiian Pineapple appliqué pattern. Enlarge pattern to fit your needs.

Pineapple Quilting
by Dixie Haywood

It has been my experience that people are intimidated by the prospect of quilting a Pineapple quilt because of the many seams and because choosing a quilting pattern for such a strong graphic design seems daunting. I'd like to offer the following suggestions:

While quilting in the ditch is useful for defining the patches it is not satisfactory as the only quilting design. It will add some texture but not the richness another layer of design can add. The only place in WEBSITE, page 14, where in-the-ditch quilting was used was in the framing of the blocks at the edge of the piecing. I wanted those strips to puff up to contrast with the heavier quilting in the more important center of the quilt.

Let the graphics of the quilt help you design the quilting. For instance, in WEBSITE, I wanted to reinforce the idea that the web overlays the yellow layer, so I quilted the yellow blades with large diamonds without stitching across the webs. In the blades with hand-dyed fabrics, each strip was quilted with a diagonal line to suggest motion.

I considered, but did not use, two other quilting ideas. I thought about using double parallel quilting lines in the yellow blades and quilting curved lines from the center of the block to the tip of each hand-dyed blade. The large diamond shapes, formed when four blocks meet at their corners, were quilted with a design that suggested a web. The web theme was further reinforced by the quilting in the borders.

Hand quilting across seams can be eased by leaving a little play when putting the quilt in a frame, rather than pulling it taut, and you will be able to sew across seams more easily.

WEBSITE, detail, 53" x 53", 1997, by Dixie Haywood.

PINEAPPLE STRATA, 60" x 60", 1997, by Patricia Klem.

Curved Piecing
by Patricia Klem

In PINEAPPLE STRATA, I used curved piecing in some of the strips to contrast with the spiky Pineapple block. I do the curved piecing without using a template or a pattern, which allows me much more freedom in the design. I can use either shears or a rotary cutter to cut the curved strips.

I have two methods for making the curves. I can begin with a softly curved edge, overlapping another fabric. The bottom fabric is then cut by following the curves in the top piece (Fig. 1). Alternatively, I can overlap two fabrics by 2" to 3" and cut the curves through both fabrics at the same time (Fig. 2).

I sew the curves with a scant ¼" seam allowance. If the curve is gentle, it is not necessary to clip or notch. The piece will lie flat after pressing (Fig. 3).

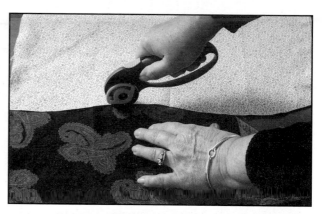

Fig. 1. Cut the curves through both fabrics at the same time.

Fig. 2. Follow the curve in the top piece to cut the bottom layer.

Fig. 3. Gentle curves will lie flat after being sewn even if you don't clip the seam allowances. PHOTOS: CAROL RICHARDSON

Here is a drawing of PINEAPPLE STRATA for you to enlarge and color.

PINEAPPLE STRATA, detail, by Patricia Klem.

Curved Piecing, Patricia Klem

Palm Frond Pattern
by Anne Oliver

PINEAPPLE PLANTATION seemed too hard-edged for me when I finished it, so I decided to soften the edges with palm fronds. The quilt measures 63" x 50", and the fronds spill out of a 5" border.

Each frond was made in three sections. Like little pillows, two layers of fabric were sewn right sides together and turned right side out. A portion of the seam was left unsewn, so that I could stuff the sections loosely with batting. The hole was sewn closed, and the sections were machine stitched to the quilt with a zigzag along the veins in the leaves. The stitching goes through all three layers.

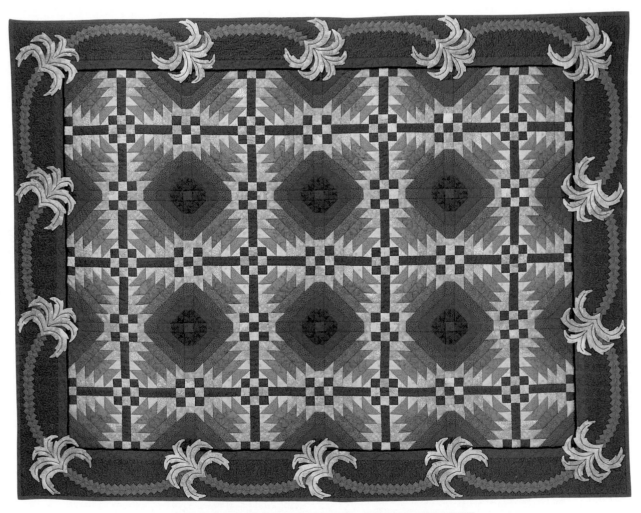

ANNE'S PINEAPPLE PLANTATION: HOW DID THE NINE PATCHES GET IN THERE?, 63" x 50", 1996, by Anne Oliver.

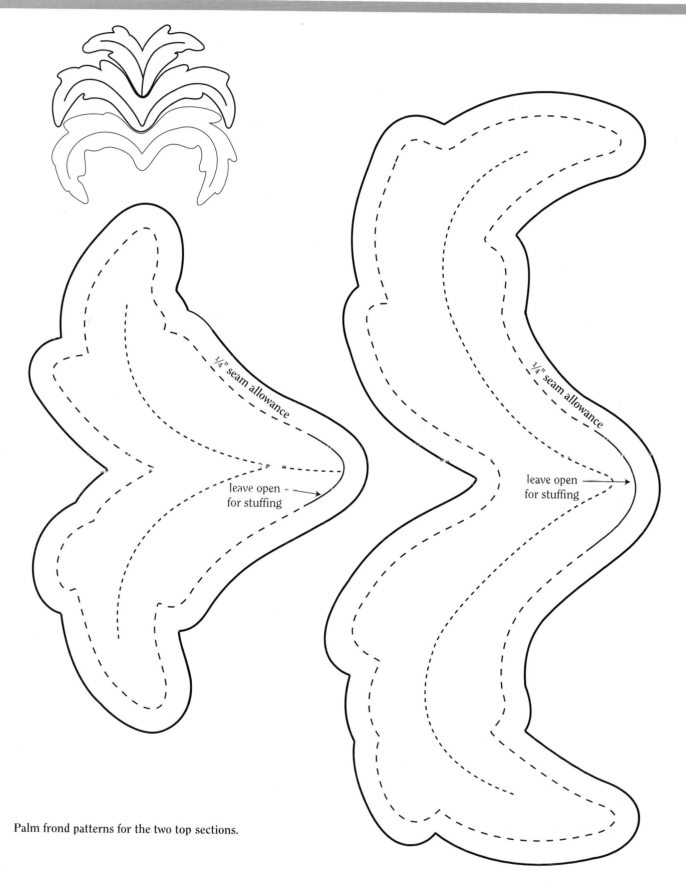

¼" seam allowance

¼" seam allowance

leave open
for stuffing

leave open
for stuffing

Palm frond patterns for the two top sections.

Palm Frond Pattern, Anne Oliver

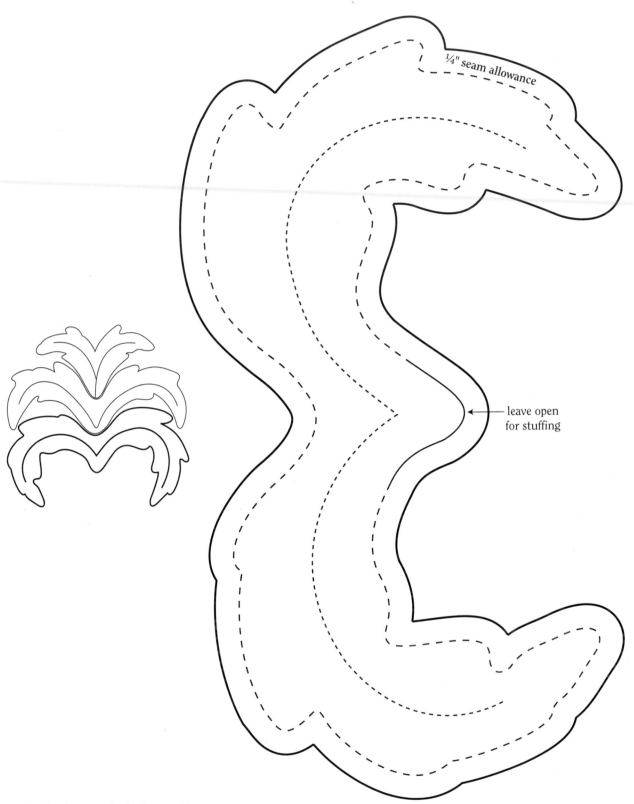

¼" seam allowance

leave open
for stuffing

Palm frond pattern for the bottom section.

Elongated Blocks
by Shirley Robinson Davis

For my quilt KILAUEA, I designed an elongated Pineapple block on the computer. I used 20 of these distorted blocks as sashing for five large Pineapple blocks set on point. Four small Pineapple blocks were used as setting squares, and the elongated blocks were repeated in the border. To try various colorations, you can photocopy the quilt design on page 87, at any convenient size. To make your own version of this quilt, follow the instructions beginning on the next page. Paper piecing patterns are on pages 88–90.

KILAUEA, 63¾" x 63¾", 1997, by Shirley Robinson Davis.

YARDAGE FOR KILAUEA
Quilt size: 63¾" x 63¾"

Position	Yards	Instruction
Blocks		Use scraps, sorted into lights, mediums, and dark
Background	⅝	
Side triangles		Cut a 9½" square in half diagonally
Corner triangles		Cut an 18½" square on both diagonals
Inner border		
Pieced	⅜	Cut six 1½" x 42" strips selvage to selvage
OR unpieced	1¾	Cut four 1½" x 55" strips parallel to selvage
Backing	4	Two panels 35" x 69"
Binding	⅝	Cut 7 strips, selvage to selvage, 2½" wide for double-fold binding (finishes approx. ⅜" wide)

ASSEMBLY

• Photocopy the paper-piecing patterns. You will need a copy for every block in the quilt. To use these patterns, place the fabric under the pattern and sew on the line on the front of the pattern. Keep in mind that this method produces a reverse image. If you are new to paper piecing, see Jane Hall's description of foundation piecing beginning on page 92.

• Dig into your scrap basket to sew the three sizes of paper-foundation-pieced blocks: Make five 12" blocks, eight 6" blocks, eight 6" half blocks, sixteen 6" x 12" blocks for the quilt body, and sixteen 6" x 12" blocks for the border.

• Cut the side and corner triangles from the background fabric as instructed in the yardage chart. Sew the triangles, sashing, and setting squares (6" blocks) together in diagonal rows; then sew the rows together.

• Cut the border strips. If you cut the inner border strips from selvage to selvage, sew all the strips together, end to end and cut them into four equal lengths. Whether strips are pieced or unpieced, sew two strips to the sides of the quilt. Trim off the extra length even with the quilt's edges. Sew the remaining two strips to the top and bottom of the quilt and trim as before.

• Measure the quilt to determine the length needed for the pieced borders. Sew four elongated blocks together, end to end, to make one border strip and measure its length. If the measurements differ, make adjustments by adding or subtracting equal amounts in the seams between the elongated blocks. Make three more border strips. Sew a border strip to each side of the quilt. Then sew a corner block to each end of one of the remaining strips and sew this strip to the top of the quilt. Repeat for the bottom of the quilt.

• Sew the two backing panels together along their length. Layer the quilt top, batting, and backing and baste the layers together with thread or safety pins. Quilt as desired before binding your Pineapple masterpiece.

Quilt design to enlarge and color.

Elongated Blocks, Shirley Robinson Davis

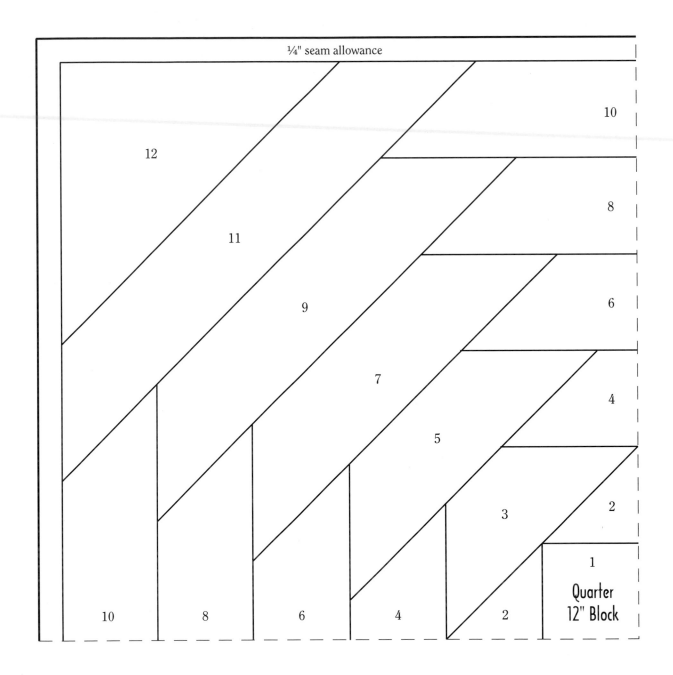

¼" seam allowance

10

12

8

11

6

9

4

7

5

2

3

1

2

Quarter
12" Block

10   8   6   4   2

KILAUEA block pattern.

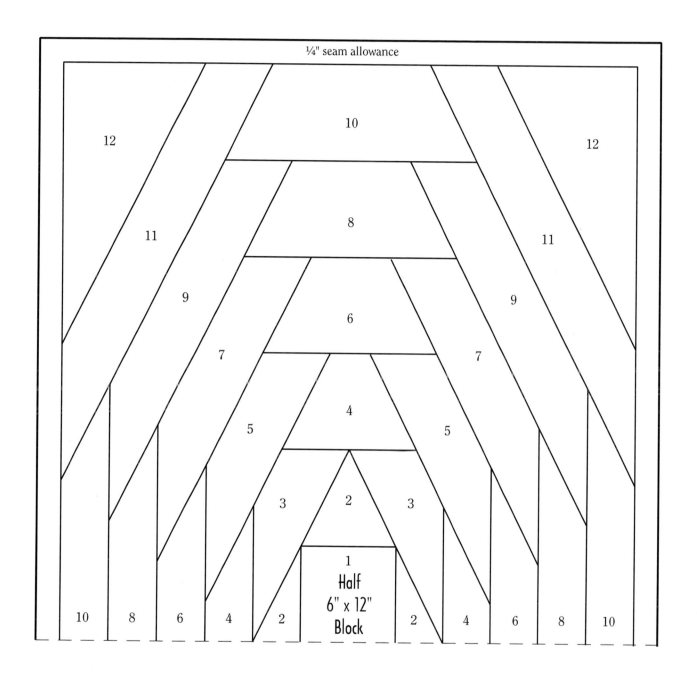

¼" seam allowance

10

12   12

11   11

8

9   9

6

7   7

4

5   5

3   2   3

1
Half
6" x 12"
Block

10   8   6   4   2   2   4   6   8   10

KILAUEA elongated block pattern.

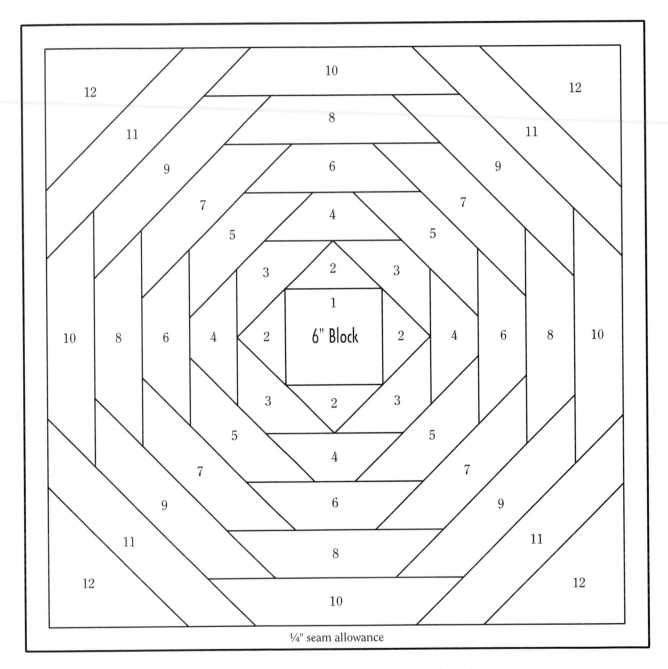

These 6" blocks were used as "setting squares" in the sashing formed by the elongated blocks.

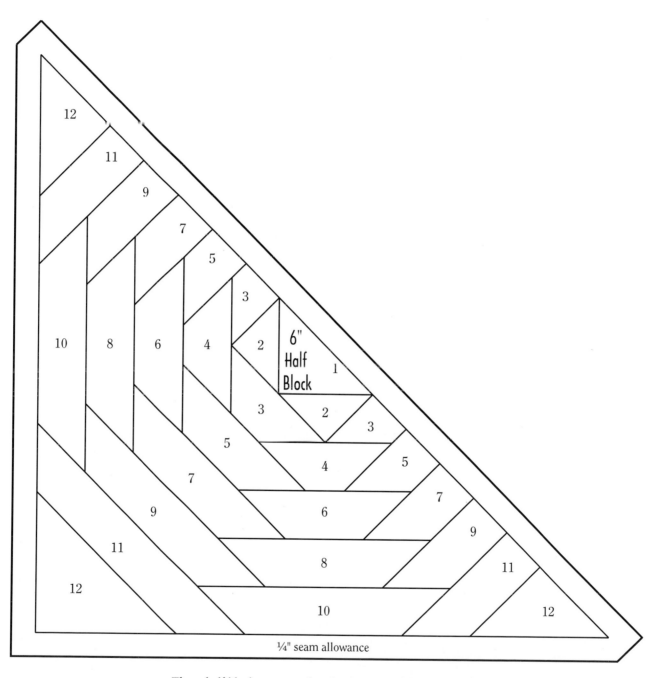

Numbers in the diagram: 12, 11, 9, 7, 5, 3, 2, 1 — 6" Half Block — 3, 2, 3, 4, 5, 7, 9, 11, 12 and 10, 8, 6, 4, 5, 7, 9, 11, 12

¼" seam allowance

These half blocks were used as "setting triangle" in the sashing formed by the elongated blocks.

Elongated Blocks, *Shirley Robinson Davis*

Foundation Piecing
by Jane Hall

CHROMA VI: NEBULA, 58" x 58", 1997, by Jane C. Hall.

I recommend piecing this traditional Pineapple block with a foundation. If you are going to piece by hand, use either a lightweight fabric, such as muslin, or a removable interfacing for the foundation. If you are piecing by machine, use tracing paper or a lightweight removable interfacing.

Trace the pattern accurately with a sharp pencil. If you use tracing paper, you can make multiple foundations by needle punching the original pattern with an unthreaded sewing machine (up to 10 sheets at a time). If you use interfacing or muslin, each pattern must be traced individually.

Classically, the strips in the diagonal blades are made with dark fabric and those in the horizontal and vertical blades with light fabric. The Pineapple block relies on a sharp value contrast between the blades to create the familiar secondary star and windmill designs. You can make all the strips in a blade from one fabric, or you can use a mix of fabrics in the same value.

To make a block, cut a square of fabric for the center and cut strips of light and dark fabrics for the blades. Pin the center square of fabric, right side up, on the back side of the foundation. Make sure the fabric square overlaps the drawn lines by at least ¼" on all sides. (You will need backlighting from a window or a lamp, so you can see through the foundation to center the square within the lines on the front of the foundation.)

Cut four pieces from the first light strip, each the length of a side of the center fabric square. Pin one of the light pieces on the center fabric square, right sides together, being careful to position the pin away from the sewing line (Fig. 1). Use a slightly shorter stitch length than usual, about 14–16 stitches to the inch. Turn the foundation over and, with the fabric against the feed dogs, sew on the seam line between the square and the first piece, beginning and ending two stitches beyond the line (Fig. 2). By stitching a bit beyond the line, you won't have to lock the stitches because they will be locked in place by subsequent rows. Trim the seam allowance to ¼", if necessary (Fig. 3, page 94). Finger press the piece open, and pin it in place (Fig. 4, page 94).

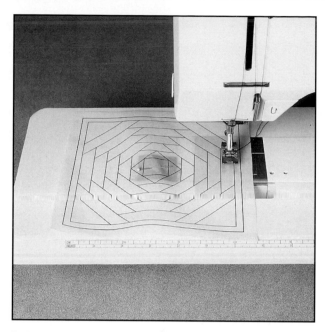

fig. 1. Pin the first two pieces on the back of the pattern. Be sure that you have enough seam allowance all around.

fig. 2. Begin and end one or two stitches beyond the line.

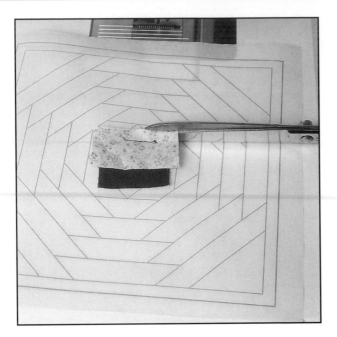

Fig. 3. Trim the seam allowance to ¼", if necessary.

Fig. 4. Finger press the piece open, and pin it in place.

To help keep the center square, sew the second piece to the opposite side. Pin, stitch, trim, press, and pin as before. Sew two more pieces to the remaining sides of the square to complete a row.

Cut four pieces from the first dark strip, cutting them ½" longer than the first diagonal stitching line. Measure against the seam lines on the front of the foundation. Position a piece, right side down on the first diagonal line and pin. Turn the foundation over, stitch on the line, turn the foundation back to the fabric side; finger press and pin the piece open. Sew the next piece on the opposite side of the block. Continue adding pieces in this manner. If you like, you can pin and stitch the two opposite pieces at the same time without cutting the threads or removing the foundation from the machine. Just raise the presser foot and drag the threads to the second piece. Lower the needle and presser foot, and sew. The loops of thread can be cut off at the surface after each group of four has been sewn.

Leave the pins in place until the next row has been sewn, to keep the strips flat. After the fifth row, it will be possible to pin and sew all four strips at the same time without cutting the threads or removing the block from the machine. After the four pieces have been sewn, clip the threads and remove the block. The rest of the rows can be sewn in this manner.

The final pieces for the corners of the block can be made from a wider strip cut the height of the triangle plus ½" for allowances. Give the block a final pressing and stay-stitch the outer strips to the foundation by sewing around the block just inside the seam allowance. Keep the foundations in place until the blocks have been joined and the borders added.

To learn more about foundation piecing techniques for Pineapple quilts, see *Perfect Pineapples* (C&T, 1989), by Jane Hall and Dixie Haywood.

Broken Arrow Border
by Linda Juniér

Like Shirley Davis, Linda Juniér used a computer program to make an elongated Pineapple block for her quilt BROKEN ARROW. Here is Linda's version in a 5" x 10" size. You can see the difference color placement makes if you compare Linda's (page 32) and Shirley's (Kilauea, page 24) quilts.

To make a quilt like BROKEN ARROW, make 18 of the 5" x 10" elongated blocks and sew them together in six straight rows of three blocks each. Then follow the border assembly instructions on the next page to add the three borders. The quilt will finish approximately 46" x 46".

BROKEN ARROW, 55½" x 56", 1997, by Linda Juniér.

BORDER ASSEMBLY

Border patches can be rotary cut, or you can make traditional templates from the patch patterns provided on pages 97 and 98.

• Take a moment to study the border assembly diagram and the quilt photo. For an inner border strip, sew six light and five dark A patches together. Make four of these strips. Sew all four to the quilt and add the corner B patches to complete the inner border.

• For the middle border, cut strips 1½" wide (1" wide finished) and at least 39" long. Sew two strips to opposite sides of the quilt and trim off the extra length even with the raw edges of the quilt. Repeat for the top and bottom of the quilt.

• The outer border is made in units. Refer to the border assembly diagram below for patch orientation and sew the light and medium C patches together. You will need 28 of these triangle units. Add the D patches to the triangles to complete the square unit. Sew the square units together in groups of seven to make the four border strips. Sew two border strips to the sides of the quilt. For the corner squares, sew a light D patch to a dark D patch. Make 4 corner squares. Sew a corner square to each end of the two remaining border strips, and sew the strips to the top and bottom of the quilt.

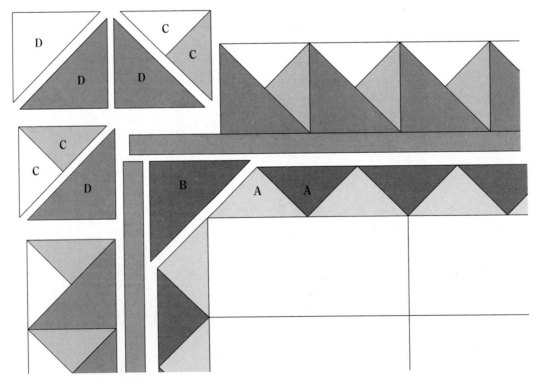

Border assembly.

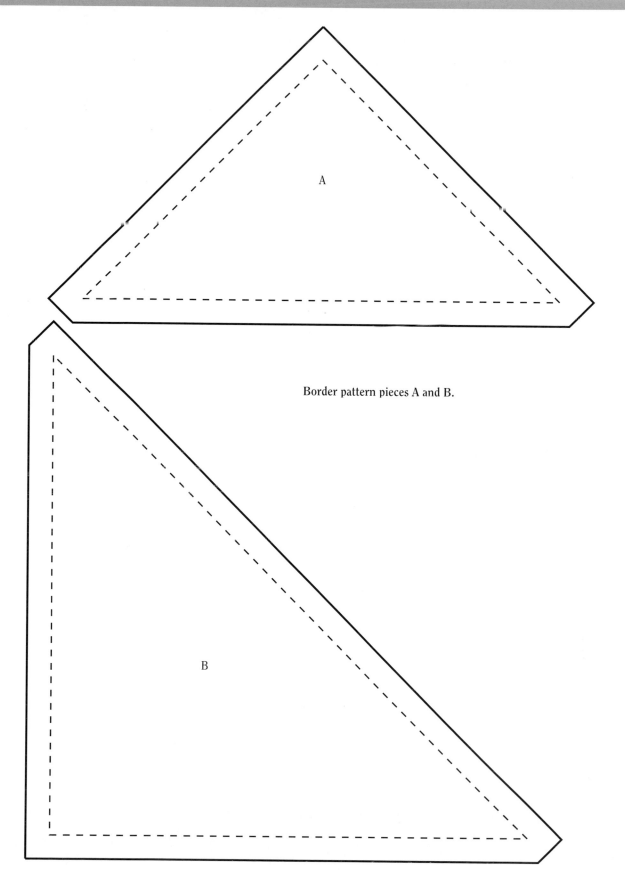

A

Border pattern pieces A and B.

B

Broken Arrow Border, Linda Juniér

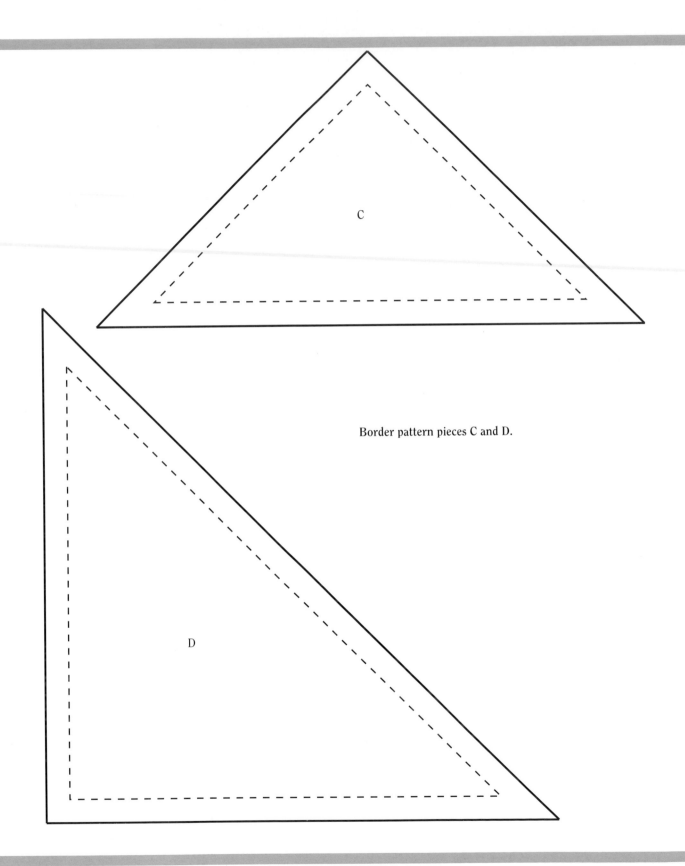

C

D

Border pattern pieces C and D.

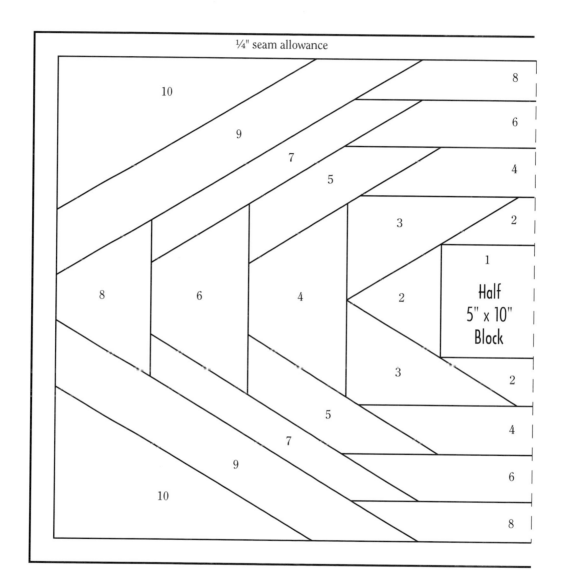

¼" seam allowance

10   8

9   6

7   4

5   3   2

1

8   6   4   2

Half
5" x 10"
Block

3

2

5   4

7   6

9   8

10

Linda's elongated block pattern.

Pineapple Tips

DESIGNING

A traditional Pineapple relies on sharp value contrasts between the diagonal and the horizontal and vertical planes to create the familiar secondary star and windmill designs. When you look at a black-and-white design sheet containing multiple Pineapple blocks, it is easy to see classic as well as non-traditional designs within the Pineapple format. Borders for Pineapple blocks can be built in, either extending or containing the center design.

FOUNDATION PIECING

Use a glue stick to attach the first fabric square to the center of a paper pattern....*Armida James*

Since my blocks for CRUSHED PINEAPPLE were too large to reproduce on a copier, I made copies of the master by perforating paper with my sewing machine and an unthreaded needle. The paper foundations gave me the freedom to ignore fabric grain line, and they simplified the cutting....*Judy Sogn*

To determine the width of a strip to cut for paper piecing, measure the pattern strip width and add a ½" seam allowance. Also, using a #14 needle with a very short stitch will perforate the paper and make it easier to remove....*Linda Juniér*

Foundation piecing was the main technique I used in PINEAPPLE STRATA. I made my own patterns and found that newsprint paper (not newspaper—the print might rub off on your fabric) worked well. It can be found at art supply stores, but I am able to get free roll ends from our local newspaper. To help me line up the next fabric piece on the side of the pattern that did not have the sewing line, I folded the pattern and the previous fabric on the line and made a crease with my finger. Then, I could line up the next fabric piece just slightly overlapping the crease....*Sherri Bain Driver*

PHOTO: CAROL RICHARDSON

To avoid bulk in a large quilt, I remove the foundation paper as I go, but I make sure the outer edges of each block retain the paper for an accurate stitching line in sewing the blocks together....*Lois Monieson*

To remove paper from paper-pieced blocks, crease it to make it easier to tear away....*Armida James*

Here is another hint to help you remove foundation paper. Place a small ruler on the paper stitching line and go over the line with a seam ripper. The paper comes off much easier....*Lois Monieson*

QUILTING DESIGN

I designed the leaf spray quilting for LEAF FALL by ironing a piece of freezer paper to the finished quilt top and sketching curves and ovals until I liked the results. It helps in drawing if you hold your pencil by the eraser end and keep your wrist floppy. Use a permanent marker and go over the design lines you like best.... *Gertrude Embree*

To make a quilting pattern for LEAF FALL, I laid a heavy see-through plastic over the top of the quilt while it was mounted on a design wall. I then doodled quilting designs on the plastic. When the design was pleasing to the eye, I transferred it to pieces of wax paper. The design was quartered diagonally and pinned to the quilt top. I then quilted through the paper, a quarter at a time.... *Gayle Wallace*

QUILTING

For machine quilting with nylon thread in the needle and a different thread in the bobbin, don't forget to loosen the top tension. The top and bottom threads need to interlock in the middle of the batting layer. Use a small sample of fabric and batting layers to test the locking of the stitches.... *Marta Amundson*

The Quiltmakers

The Quilts

AQS BOOKS ON QUILTS

This is only a partial listing of the books on quilts that are available from the American Quilter's Society. AQS books are known the world over for their timely topics, clear writing, beautiful color photographs, and accurate illustrations and patterns. The following books are available from your local bookseller, quilt shop, or public library. If you are unable to locate certain titles in your area, you may order by mail from the AMERICAN QUILTER'S SOCIETY, P.O. Box 3290, Paducah, KY 42002-3290. Add $2.00 for postage for the first book ordered and 40¢ for each additional book. Include item number, title, and price when ordering. Allow 14 to 21 days for delivery. Customers with Visa, MasterCard, or Discover may phone in orders from 7:00–5:00 CST, Monday–Friday, Toll Free 1-800-626-5420.

4595	**Above & Beyond Basics**, Karen Kay Buckley	$18.95
2282	**Adapting Architectural Details for Quilts**, Carol Wagner	$12.95
4813	**Addresses & Birthdays**, compiled by Klaudeen Hansen (HB)	$14.95
4543	**American Quilt Blocks: 50 Patterns for 50 States**, Beth Summers	$16.95
4696	**Amish Kinder Komforts**, Bettina Havig	$14.95
4829	**Anita Shackelford: Surface Textures**, Anita Shackelford (HB)	$24.95
4899	**Appliqué Paper Greetings**, Elly Sienkiewicz (HB)	$24.95
3790	**Appliqué Patterns from Native American Beadwork Designs**, Dr. Joyce Mori	$14.95
2099	**Ask Helen: More About Quilting Designs**, Helen Squire	$14.95
2207	**Award-Winning Quilts: 1985-1987**	$24.95
2354	**Award-Winning Quilts: 1988-1989**	$24.95
3425	**Award-Winning Quilts: 1990-1991**	$24.95
3791	**Award-Winning Quilts: 1992-1993**	$24.95
4830	**Baskets: Celtic Style**, Scarlett Rose	$19.95
4832	**A Batch of Patchwork**, May T. Miller & Susan B. Burton	$18.95
4593	**Blossoms by the Sea: Making Ribbon Flowers for Quilts**, Faye Labanaris	$24.95
4898	**Borders & Finishing Touches**, Bonnie K. Browning	$16.95
4697	**Caryl Bryer Fallert: A Spectrum of Quilts, 1983-1995**, Caryl Bryer Fallert	$24.95
4626	**Celtic Geometric Quilts**, Camille Remme	$16.95
3926	**Celtic Style Floral Appliqué**, Scarlett Rose	$14.95
2208	**Classic Basket Quilts**, Elizabeth Porter & Marianne Fons	$16.95
2355	**Creative Machine Art**, Sharee Dawn Roberts	$24.95
4818	**Dear Helen, Can You Tell Me?** Helen Squire	$15.95
3399	**Dye Painting!** Ann Johnston	$19.95
4814	**Encyclopedia of Designs for Quilting**, Phyllis D. Miller (HB)	$34.95
3468	**Encyclopedia of Pieced Quilt Patterns**, compiled by Barbara Brackman	$34.95
3846	**Fabric Postcards**, Judi Warren	$22.95
4594	**Firm Foundations**, Jane Hall & Dixie Haywood	$18.95
4900	**Four Blocks Continued…**, Linda Giesler Carlson	$16.95
2381	**From Basics to Binding**, Karen Kay Buckley	$16.95
4526	**Gatherings: America's Quilt Heritage**, Kathlyn F. Sullivan	$34.95
2097	**Heirloom Miniatures**, Tina M. Gravatt	$9.95
4628	**Helen's Guide to quilting in the 21st century**, Helen Squire	$16.95
1906	**Irish Chain Quilts: A Workbook of Irish Chains**, Joyce B. Peaden	$14.95
3784	**Jacobean Appliqué: Book I, "Exotica,"** Campbell & Ayars	$18.95
4544	**Jacobean Appliqué: Book II, "Romantica,"** Campbell & Ayars	$18.95
3904	**The Judge's Task**, Patricia J. Morris	$19.95
4751	**Liberated Quiltmaking**, Gwen Marston (HB)	$24.95
4897	**Lois Smith's Machine Quiltmaking**, Lois Smith	$19.95
4523	**Log Cabin Quilts: New Quilts from an Old Favorite**	$14.95
4545	**Log Cabin with a Twist**, Barbara T. Kaempfer	$18.95
4815	*Love to Quilt:* **Bears, Bears, Bears**, Karen Kay Buckley	$14.95
4833	*Love to Quilt:* **Broderie Perse: The Elegant Quilt**, Barbara W. Barber	$14.95
4598	*Love to Quilt:* **Men's Vests**, Alexandra Capadalis Dupré	$14.95
4816	*Love to Quilt:* **Necktie Sampler Blocks**, Janet B. Elwin	$14.95
4753	*Love to Quilt:* **Penny Squares**, Willa Baranowski	$12.95
4911	**Mariner's Compass Quilts: New Quilts from an Old Favorite**	$16.95
4752	**Miniature Quilts: Connecting New & Old Worlds**, Tina M. Gravatt	$14.95
4514	**Mola Techniques for Today's Quilters**, Charlotte Patera	$18.95
3330	**More Projects and Patterns**, Judy Florence	$18.95
1981	**Nancy Crow: Quilts and Influences**, Nancy Crow	$29.95
3331	**Nancy Crow: Work in Transition**, Nancy Crow	$12.95
4828	**Nature, Design & Silk Ribbons**, Cathy Grafton	$18.95
3332	**New Jersey Quilts**, The Heritage Quilt Project of New Jersey	$29.95
3927	**New Patterns from Old Architecture**, Carol Wagner	$12.95
2153	**No Dragons on My Quilt**, Jean Ray Laury	$12.95
4627	**Ohio Star Quilts: New Quilts from an Old Favorite**	$16.95
3469	**Old Favorites in Miniature**, Tina Gravatt	$15.95
4831	**Optical Illusions for Quilters**, Karen Combs	$22.95
4515	**Paint and Patches: Painting on Fabrics with Pigment**, Vicki L. Johnson	$18.95
4513	**Plaited Patchwork**, Shari Cole	$19.95
3928	**Precision Patchwork for Scrap Quilts**, Jeannette Tousley Muir	$12.95
4779	**Protecting Your Quilts: A Guide for Quilt Owners, Second Edition**	$6.95
4542	**A Quilted Christmas**, edited by Bonnie Browning	$18.95
2380	**Quilter's Registry**, Lynne Fritz	$9.95
3467	**Quilting Patterns from Native American Designs**, Dr. Joyce Mori	$12.95
3470	**Quilting with Style**, Gwen Marston & Joe Cunningham	$24.95
2284	**Quiltmaker's Guide: Basics & Beyond**, Carol Doak	$19.95
4918	**Quilts by Paul D. Pilgrim: Blending the Old & the New**, Gerald E. Roy	$16.95
2257	*Quilts:* **The Permanent Collection – MAQS**	$9.95
3793	*Quilts:* **The Permanent Collection – MAQS Volume II**	$9.95
3789	**Roots, Feathers & Blooms**, Linda Giesler Carlson	$16.95
4512	**Sampler Quilt Blocks from Native American Designs**, Dr. Joyce Mori	$14.95
3796	**Seasons of the Heart & Home: Quilts for a Winter's Day**, Jan Patek	$18.95
3761	**Seasons of the Heart & Home: Quilts for Summer Days**, Jan Patek	$18.95
2357	**Sensational Scrap Quilts**, Darra Duffy Williamson	$24.95
4783	**Silk Ribbons by Machine**, Jeanie Sexton	$15.95
3929	**The Stori Book of Embellishing**, Mary Stori	$16.95
3903	**Straight Stitch Machine Appliqué**, Letty Martin	$16.95
3792	**Striplate Piecing**, Debra Wagner	$24.95
3930	**Tessellations & Variations**, Barbara Ann Caron	$14.95
3788	**Three-Dimensional Appliqué**, Anita Shackelford	$24.95
4596	**Ties, Ties, Ties: Traditional Quilts from Neckties**, Janet B. Elwin	$19.95
3931	**Time-Span Quilts: New Quilts from Old Tops**, Becky Herdle	$16.95
4919	**Transforming Fabric**, Carolyn Dahl	$29.95
2029	**A Treasury of Quilting Designs**, Linda Goodmon Emery	$14.95
3847	**Tricks with Chintz**, Nancy S. Breland	$14.95
2286	**Wonderful Wearables: A Celebration of Creative Clothing**, Virginia Avery	$24.95
4812	**Who's Who in American Quilting**, edited by Bonnie Browning (HB)	$49.95
4956	**Variegreat! New Dimensions in Traditional Quilts**, Linda Glantz	$19.95
4972	**20th Century Quilts**, Cuesta Benberry and Joyce Gross	$9.95